THE
BERNARD SHAW
COMPANION

GEORGE BERNARD SHAW
AT HIS LONDON FLAT, JUNE 1935

THE
BERNARD SHAW
COMPANION

Michael and Mollie Hardwick

ST MARTIN'S PRESS
NEW YORK

FOREWORD

Like its predecessors, *The Sherlock Holmes Companion* and *The Charles Dickens Companion*, this book is intended to be both a reference work for its subject's enthusiasts, and a sampler for others prepared to sniff the bouquet and judge whether the vintage will suit their palate. Perhaps we should declare our own position: we are wholehearted aficionados of Holmes and his creator; intense admirers of Dickens's works, if not entirely of the author himself; but about Bernard Shaw we confess to ambivalence.

Without doubt, Shaw was one of the greatest of English-language dramatists. In virtually everything he wrote for the stage there is much to admire and by which to be amused. Not so often, though, do we find ourselves emotionally moved by Shaw; and we are of that number, not much catered for by the theatre today, who hope to be moved. Little wonder, then, that we believe Shaw attained his zenith with *Saint Joan* and *Heartbreak House*, the plays in which he draws nearest to that human compassion which his public pose denied. We venture to think he would have agreed with us. We think, as others have done, that that too-clever-to-be-true image disguised a shy, sensitive, un-fulfilled human being, self-buried by mounds of verbiage, political and literary attitudinising, and seemingly outrageous self-assurance.

People in other countries—and they are many, in many countries—can admire Shaw objectively for his professional skill and intellectual coruscation. We Britons find it less easy. The British public requires humility in its artists; they must know their place, with the rest of the hired players. Even if one of them is a sorcerer, like W. S. Gilbert's John Wellington Wells, he is expected to come bowing and hand-rubbing, to ask, 'I trust my conduct meets your approbation'; for us, like the pompous Alexis Pointdextre, condescendingly to reply, 'Sir, you have acted with discrimination, and shown more delicate appreciation than we expect in persons of your station'.

If ever a sorcerer transgressed, it was Shaw. He insisted on assessing his own worth, and was impenitent when rebuked. He was too clever, too witty, too prolific, too versatile—a quality much deplored in this country—too cocky by far. We suspected something of the charlatan about him. He proclaimed socialism, yet drove about in a Rolls Royce and left a fortune in six figures when he died. He affected to consider himself greater than Shakespeare (though he qualified the claim). He castigated us for eating flesh, drinking alcohol, taking tobacco, and imagining that sex is an important pleasure; expecting us, it would seem, to need nothing in life that was not sufficient for a rich, pampered, intellectual ascetic. It was cause for some glee that, after his death, there began to emerge the details of his own sexual relationships, and rumours that he had been kept going in his last days with unsuspected doses of meat-derivatives and whisky-laced soup. We drew a little closer to him for that.

In short, our impression of people's attitude towards Shaw confirms our own: we admire him greatly, but do not love him. We find him unsentimental, anti-luxurious, and maybe a bit devious; and even if he wasn't English at all, but Irish, and wasn't at heart what he chose to show himself to be, we find it hard to banish all reservations. We feel that, had we had dealings with him, he would have made us feel inferior. To be aware that this is the truth of it, anyway, and that he might well have been as charming and kind to us as he proved to many other intellectual inferiors, doesn't help.

Be this as it may, Shaw, as an artist, is established for ever. His ideas, his characters, his wit are of that substance which will keep perhaps a dozen of his plays alive, as the success of recent revivals has shown. The more one sees of them, and reads about him, especially within his own correspondence, the more that seemingly impregnable façade begins to fade and the fallible human being behind it is revealed in growing attractiveness. The assembling of this small bag of samples from his immense body of work has helped us towards him: we hope the result will do the same for a few others.

The book has the same contents as others in our 'Companion' series: a *Who's Who* of characters, plots, quotations, chronology of main works and a brief life. The fact that he held strong views about the reform of English spelling is well known, and in quoting him we have retained the forms he preferred. Our material is drawn almost entirely from the plays. Shaw wrote five unsuccessful novels before turning away from that form for good, and the novel has no more place in his achievement than the play had in Dickens's. He wrote prolifically on political and social questions; but this work is a Companion, not a Concordance, and we have concentrated upon the Shaw likely to be encountered by the public at large today. Details of his essays, preface-subjects and other writings are handily available in A. C. Ward's pamphlet *Bernard Shaw*, published for the British Council and the National Book League's series of supplements to *British Book News*. The fullest information about the plays and other dramatic versions is contained in Raymond Mander and Joe Mitchenson's *Theatrical Companion to the Plays of Shaw* (Rockliff, 1954).

We are indebted to the Society of Authors, acting on behalf of the Shaw Estate, for permission to quote freely from his works; and to Miss Audrey Williamson, author of *Bernard Shaw: Man and Writer* (Collier–Macmillan, 1963) for advice and assistance.

MICHAEL AND MOLLIE HARDWICK

CONTENTS

CHRONOLOGY OF GEORGE BERNARD SHAW'S WORKS

———◆———

Dates shown against plays are of completion of writing. Other works listed are ones in volume form only, or short works of significance, but do not include collections of the plays.

1899   CAPTAIN BRASSBOUND'S CONVERSION: *Play*

1900   LOVE AMONG THE ARTISTS: *Novel*

1901   THE ADMIRABLE BASHVILLE: *Play*

1903   MAN AND SUPERMAN: *Play*

1904   JOHN BULL'S OTHER ISLAND: *Play*

1904   HOW HE LIED TO HER HUSBAND: *Play*

1904   THE COMMON SENSE OF MUNICIPAL TRADING: *Social comment*

1905   THE IRRATIONAL KNOT: *Novel*

1905   MAJOR BARBARA: *Play*

1905   PASSION, POISON, AND PETRIFACTION: *Play*

1906   DRAMATIC OPINIONS AND ESSAYS selected by James Huneker from Shaw's theatre notes in the *Saturday Review*, introduced by Shaw

1906   THE DOCTOR'S DILEMMA: *Play*

1908   THE SANITY OF ART: *Criticism*

1908   GETTING MARRIED: *Play*

1909   THE SHEWING-UP OF BLANCO POSNET: *Play*

1909   PRESS CUTTINGS: *Play*

1909   THE FASCINATING FOUNDLING: *Play*

1909   THE GLIMPSE OF REALITY: *Play*

PLOTS OF THE PLAYS

INDEX TO PLOTS

———◆———

*. . . you can get higher rents letting by the room
than you can for a mansion in Park Lane.*

Dr. Harry Trench and an older man, Cokane, are travelling
together and at an hotel on the Rhine meet Sartorius, a self-
made rich landlord, and his daughter Blanche. Blanche and
Harry have already struck up an unconventional acquain-
tance without introduction and she is well aware he is
attracted by her. She leads him on to propose marriage,
and her father agrees, although with the proviso that
Trench guarantees his aristocratic relatives will accept
Blanche into the family.

Back in London, Sartorius's rent collector, Lickcheese,
reports that the Sanitary Inspector has been complaining
about the slum property he owns, and Sartorius threatens
to silence him. He also opposes Lickcheese's suggestions
to repair the slums, and sacks him. Harry Trench arrives
with the required letters from his relatives, and Lickcheese
appeals to him to speak to Sartorius about his dismissal.
Trench learns of Sartorius's harshness to his slum tenants.
He is also appalled by Lickcheese's revelations of the
things he has done in Sartorius's name and refuses to help
him. He tells Blanche he cannot take any of her father's
money: they will be poor, as his income is small; but she
does not know the source of her wealth or his reasons, and
they quarrel. She breaks off the engagement, and when challenged Trench accuses Sartorius to his face of slum landlordism. Sartorius reveals that the mortgage from which
Trench derives his own small income is on the same slum
property. Trench realises that people who live in glass
houses cannot throw stones, and Sartorius offers to persuade Blanche to renew the engagement. Blanche, however, is still bitterly angry, and Sartorius has to tell
Trench that she still refuses to marry him.

The following winter Lickcheese returns, now rich and

successful, having invested in properties due for government takeover with compensation. He suggests Sartorius might reap a similar harvest by improving his slum properties, to fetch higher compensation. Blanche sees Lickcheese's account book and realises where her father's money comes from. When Trench comes to the house he is now resigned to accept the scheme of Sartorius and Lickcheese, but cannot afford to risk his own income in the improvements. This is settled by his marrying Blanche, who is equally willing to put financial gain before sympathy for the poor who will be turned out of the properties.

THE PHILANDERER (1893)

A lady and gentleman are making love to one another in the drawing room of a flat in Ashley Gardens in the Victoria district of London.

The lady is a young widow, Grace Tranfield, in love with the man, Leonard Charteris, who is the 'philanderer' of the title. Grace is shocked and disconcerted to find that Charteris, on his own light-hearted admission, has been in a similar position with Julia Craven and others. The affair with Julia, in fact, has never been broken off. He maintains that it is not his fault that half the women he speaks to fall in love with him; and he is in full flight of cajolery when Julia Craven herself erupts on to the scene, attacks Grace, and announces her intention of staying until Charteris has given her up.

Charteris gets Grace out of the room and unsuccessfully reminds Julia of her supposedly advanced views on marriage. She changes from belligerence to pleading tears, without effect, and, to the consternation of both, the fathers of Grace and Julia enter together. Colonel Craven is suffering from a liver complaint, and much to Charteris' impatience 'has fully made up his mind not to survive next

Easter', just to oblige the doctors. Cuthbertson, Grace's father, is a dramatic critic and theatrically shocked to discover something of the Charteris-Grace-Julia triangle; but Charteris explains it is Grace whom he wants to marry.

The scene changes to the Ibsen Club, of which most of the characters are members. A fashionable physician, Dr. Paramore, says he has made a discovery concerning Col. Craven's fatal complaint, but horrifies Craven's younger daughter Sylvia by his practice of vivisection. Craven turns up at Cuthbertson's invitation, and Charteris outrages both men by admitting he had lied to them last night: the truth is, both young women want to marry him, but he does not want to marry either.

Julia enters the Club with Paramore dancing attendance, and manages to trap Charteris alone. She is, however, forced to retire by Sylvia, who delights Charteris by saying Dr. Paramore is in love with Julia. Charteris attempts to flirt with Grace again but is repulsed, and attention is diverted by the distraught Dr. Paramore who has learnt in the *British Medical Journal* that his 'discovery', Craven's liver complaint, is a disease which doesn't exist. He complains of lack of animals for experiment, and resents Craven's delight at learning he is not to die. Charteris, to cheer him, suggests that Julia is fascinated by him, but it is Grace who comes in first and retires with the doctor tête-à-tête. Changing tactics, Charteris points them out to Julia, arousing her jealousy. The result is another quarrel between Julia and Grace, who threatens to have Julia expelled from the Club. Julia hurries after Dr. Paramore, to enlist him as a witness in her favour, and Charteris tries to prevent the others following, in order to give the doctor time to propose to her.

This Paramore does, at his house, and Julia, dubious but flattered, accepts him before the others arrive. Charteris is delighted, and Julia and Grace, reconciled, congratulate each other on having escaped him. Nevertheless, Julia bitterly regrets not being brave enough to kill Charteris, and the others 'look at her with concern, and even a little awe, feeling for the first time the presence of a keen sorrow'.

MRS. WARREN'S PROFESSION (1894)

> *It is true that in Mrs. Warren's Profession, Society, and not any individual, is the villain of the piece.*

Vivie Warren, a Cambridge-educated girl advanced in her ideas, is living in a rented cottage near Haslemere. She is visited by an old friend of her mother's, Praed, who says her mother is coming down from London. Mrs. Warren has lived mainly abroad. When she arrives she is accompanied by a man-about-town, Sir George Crofts. Sir George, attracted by Vivie, enquires of Praed if he knows who Vivie's father was. Praed says he has no idea. Sir George is worried that it may be himself. A young easy-going rector's son, Frank Gardner, is also very attracted by Vivie, but it transpires that his father, the local vicar, had once written compromising letters to a woman and has told Frank the tale as a warning. When Mrs. Warren comes out of the cottage she greets the clergyman as a friend of long ago, to his obvious embarrassment.

The Rev. Samuel Gardner agitatedly warns Frank that his marriage to Vivie is out of the question but Mrs. Warren defiantly refuses to forbid it, until she learns that Frank has run through his patrimony and has no means of supporting her daughter. Frank, however, is lightheartedly persistent. Crofts reveals his own wish to marry Vivie, and Mrs. Warren is revolted. She learns from Vivie of her intention to earn her own living and is angry, but Vivie counters by pointing out that she has no idea who her father is, and that people should overcome circumstances by their own effort. Mrs. Warren tells of her own upbringing, in poverty, without a known father, until she and her sister rebelled against sweated factory labour and went on the streets. Later they ran a brothel in Brussels. She maintains that the girls were far better off than in the factory and that she was able to save for a better life.

Vivie appreciates her mother's character and point of view. Next day she accompanies her to the vicarage, where she resents Frank's criticism of her mother as a 'bad lot'. They are briefly reconciled before Frank follows his father and Mrs. Warren to the church. Crofts offers marriage to Vivie. She refuses him, and he tells how much her mother owes him: he had put £40,000 into her business. Vivie says she understands the business was long ago wound up and the money invested, but learns to her horror that it is still flourishing and is the source of her and her mother's income. Crofts is taken aback to find Vivie knows what the business is. Frank challenges him with a sporting rifle and Crofts takes his revenge by saying Vivie is his half-sister. Vivie repulses Frank and goes off to work in the legal chambers of her friend Honoria Fraser, in Chancery Lane.

Here Frank calls on her. He says he is certain he does not feel for her as a brother and does not believe they are related. Vivie agrees, but says it is the only relationship she wishes with him. Praed, on his way to Italy, comes to say goodbye and Vivie, finding him as innocent as Frank of her mother's profession, tells them both why she has left her mother for good. Frank tells Praed he cannot now think of marrying Vivie, not for moral reasons but financial ones: he could not touch Mrs. Warren's money and has none of his own.

Mrs. Warren turns up, soberly dressed, to try to win back Vivie, who has returned her month's allowance through the bank. She tries to persuade her that as the whole world is hypocritical it is stupid of her to throw away riches and the kind of life they bring. Vivie counters that she would only be bored by such a life in any case, and has no need of her mother or Frank. She forces from the tearful Mrs. Warren the reluctant agreement that in getting rid of her she is doing the right thing: they have nothing in common. 'But Lord help the world,' says Mrs. Warren, 'if everybody took to doing the right thing!' She goes, and Vivie, tearing up the note left by Frank, starts to work.

ARMS AND THE MAN (1894)

> ... *it came into my head just as he was holding me in his arms and looking into my eyes, that perhaps we only had our heroic ideas because we are so fond of reading Byron and Pushkin* ...

In a small Bulgarian town in 1885, Raina Petkoff, a young lady of rich family, is delighted and slightly surprised to hear of the heroic exploit of her fiancé, Sergius Saranoff, in leading a cavalry charge into the enemy lines and winning a battle against the Serbs. As she reads in bed a man breaks in and, at gunpoint, demands her silence and protection. He is Bluntschli, a fleeing soldier of the Serbian army. Raina, knowing her countrymen would kill him, hides him behind her curtains and lies when the balcony is searched. Left alone with him again, she learns that his revolver is not loaded: he considers chocolate creams more useful on the field of battle. She is contemptuous of his nervous fears and disbelieves his eye-witness story that Sergius led the cavalry to certain death only because his horse ran away with him, and the Bulgarians won because the Serbs had run out of ammunition which would have slaughtered the cavalry. She shows Bluntschli a photograph of her fiancé and he laughs. Nevertheless she says he is safe under the Bulgarian laws of hospitality, and fetches her mother. They find Bluntschli, who is a Swiss hotel-keeper's son and a volunteer, not a Serb, asleep on Raina's bed.

March, 1886. In the Petkoffs' garden the maid Louka is being lectured by her fiancé, the servant Nicola, who fears the effect of her independent spirit on his career. She says she knows family secrets and they wouldn't dare discharge her. Major Petkoff and Sergius return from the war and mention being outwitted in a prisoners' exchange deal by a Swiss hotelier's son in the Serbian army. They recount the Swiss's story of being hidden by two Bulgarian women who were charmed by him, sending him away disguised in an old coat belonging to the master of the house. Raina and Sergius greet each other on a note of lofty romance, but as soon as she leaves him Sergius flirts with Louka. He is jealous at Louka's hint that Raina, too, has another interest, but Louka spiritedly maintains he has shown himself to be the same clay as herself.

Bluntschli calls to return Petkoff's coat and Raina involuntarily exclaims, 'Oh! The chocolate-cream soldier!' This remark is passed off with a cock and bull story involving the unfortunate and bewildered Nicola, and Bluntschli is asked to stay, Catherine Petkoff, Raina's mother, contriving the 'discovery' of the missing coat in a cupboard.

Louka finds Nicola willing to help her ambitions with Sergius, and she points out to Sergius that her waiting on him degrades him as much as herself. She taunts him with Raina's preference for Bluntschli and practically dares Sergius to surmount social barriers and marry her. Sergius challenges Bluntschli to a duel. Raina intervenes. She gathers that Sergius has been flirting with Louka and arouses his jealousy by saying Louka is engaged to Nicola. The real attractions and the class shams thus being revealed, the way is open for Raina to pair with Bluntschli and Sergius with Louka.

CANDIDA (1895)

Thats a good bid, Eugene.

At the house of the Rev. James Morell in north-east London, his secretary Proserpine Garnett ('Prossy') is arranging lecture dates with him. He is a Christian Socialist much in demand as a speaker. His curate 'Lexy' Mill, exasperates Prossy by idealising Morell's wife Candida, whose father, Burgess, calls. He is on bad terms with Morell who resents his payment of low wages as an employer, but Burgess pretends he has reformed, although it is to get a County Council contract. Candida returns from a short holiday, bringing Eugene Marchbanks, a shy, timid poet of 18 and protégé of the Morells. Burgess is impressed to learn that despite his shabby appearance he is the nephew of a peer. Marchbanks is incredulous that Morell thinks his marriage a happy one, and obviously considers him unfit for Candida. He blurts out to Morell that he loves his wife, and Morell's self-esteem begins to be punctured by the youth's contempt. Marchbanks challenges him to let Candida know what he has said, as he believes it will open her eyes to his understanding of her: if Morell shirks it he will know to the end of his days that Candida really belongs to Marchbanks. Candida, who 'babies' Marchbanks, asks him to stay to lunch, not realising the situation.

That afternoon Marchbanks shocks Prossy with his unconventional talk and discovers her secret infatuation with Morell. He is disturbed to find that a woman can really love such a man. When Candida comes in she is amused by his idealisation of her and his distress at her soiling her hands with the lamps. She notices with concern that Morell looks strained, and reveals to him the nature of 'Prossy's complaint' and that it is himself, rather than his socialist preaching, that wins him his public following. She worries him further by saying Marchbanks needs love. Morell has sent a telegram cancelling a lecture but is persuaded to go. He insists on Candida's remaining behind with Marchbanks. Marchbanks realises he is afraid of him and of putting his claim to be the right man for Candida to the test.

Later that evening Marchbanks is still reading his poetry to Candida. He looks on it romantically as the equivalent of the legendary hero's drawn sword lying between them. Candida humours him in maternal fashion, and Morell returns to find him with his head in her lap. Candida is quite unembarrassed. When she has gone, Morell anxiously questions Marchbanks, who unintentionally gives him the impression that Candida confessed she loved him. Morell tries to shake the truth from him. He suffers when he realises the matter is still unsettled. Both men challenge Candida to decide which of them she loves. Marchbanks appeals to her protective instinct, playing up his frailty and need. 'Thats a good bid, Eugene,' she says. Morell claims he can give strength for her defence, honesty, industry and authority. But Candida only replies: 'I give myself to the weaker of the two', and Eugene, with his poet's perception, realises instantly he has lost. As she tells them, she as the wife is the strength behind Morell, who was spoiled and sustained from childhood by his parents and sisters and is now kept free for his work by her domestic care. Marchbanks, always the rebel in his home, has basically far greater strength and self-sufficiency: it is the moral strength of the writer. Marchbanks accepts this truth, and goes out to fulfil his destiny, no longer a boy, but a man.

THE MAN OF DESTINY (1895)

> *There is only one universal passion: fear ... It is fear that makes men fight: it is indifference that makes them run away: fear is the mainspring of war.*

On 12 May, 1796, two days after crossing the fire-swept bridge at Lodi, the 27-year-old general, Napoleon Bonaparte, is mapping out his Italian campaign against the Austrians in the village inn at Tavazzana. A guileless young lieutenant brings the news that he has been robbed of his horse, pistols and despatches by a youth under the guise of friendship. As he is speaking, the voice of a Strange French Lady who recently arrived at the inn is heard calling for the landlord, and the Lieutenant swears it is the youth's voice. When she enters he seizes her. She appeals to Napoleon for help, saying the youth must have been her twin brother. Napoleon, although susceptible to her beauty, demands the despatches, which he realises are hidden in her bosom. She prevaricates, with flattery and cajolery, and makes it clear she stole one particular letter to protect someone, but is forced to hand over the despatches. She subtly suggests that the letter she wished to steal is a love letter from a woman to the Director, Barras, whom Napoleon knows through his wife, and that this woman cheats men and her husband knows it. The suggestion strikes home. Napoleon offers her back the letters. She refuses them, and he puts them into his breast pocket, sends for the disgraced lieutenant and says his only chance of rehabilitating himself is to recover the despatches.

The lady secretly tells the lieutenant she can get word to her brother to come to the inn. When she comes back dressed as the boy, she openly discovers the despatches in Napoleon's pocket. As she tells Napoleon, he is outwitted; but it transpires both of them have now read the letter. But 'Caesar's wife is above suspicion' and the two burn the letter as the night deepens and hides them.

YOU NEVER CAN TELL (1896)

> *Well, Sir, you never can tell. Thats a principle of life with me, Sir.*

A young impoverished dentist, Valentine, in a new practice by the sea, has just taken out the tooth of an 18-year-old young lady, Dolly Clandon, whose twin brother Philip calls for her. The garrulous and inquisitive twins invite the dentist to lunch at their hotel. He learns that they are the children of a woman writer, Mrs. Lanfrey Clandon, of Madeira, but have no notion who their father was. Valentine regretfully points out that in an English seaside resort a father is an indispensable part of one's social equipment, and for fear of his practice he dare not lunch with them. The twins' mother and sister Gloria come in, and Valentine falls immediately in love with Gloria. While he goes to stave off the landlord, to whom he owes rent, the twins and Gloria question Mrs. Clandon about their father. She horrifies them by a tale of her husband's brutality through temper, and refuses to discuss him further. Valentine asks if he can bring his landlord to lunch (he wanted a tooth out, not the rent). Mrs. Clandon, consenting, leaves to meet an old friend at the hotel, and the rest meet the landlord, Fergus Crampton. He comments on Dolly's likeness to his mother. He apparently resents an injury done him by his family. When the girls have left, Valentine suggests he himself may want to marry soon, and provokes from Crampton a disgruntled comment on marriage in general and his own wife and three children in particular. He has no idea where they are now. He bets Valentine his arrears of rent that he will not be able to take out his tooth without hurting him, and Valentine promptly gives him gas.

On the terrace of the Marine Hotel, the waiter talks pleasantly of the Clandons to Finch M'Comas, a solicitor, the friend expected by Mrs. Clandon. When they meet, they talk of their once advanced political opinions and Mrs. Clandon's championship of women's rights, but M'Comas warns her that Gloria will be swept into socialism, the new rage, of which they both disapprove. Mrs. Clandon asks

Finch to explain the family position to the children. It transpires Crampton is their father, and the twins suggest their friend the waiter, whom they call William after Shakespeare, should break the news to him when he comes. When he does so Crampton is furious and thinks Valentine was in the plot; but the family come to meet him and Crampton is trapped into taking the head of the table. During the waiter's tactful service it transpires his son is a barrister and a Q.C. Crampton resents the freedom and lack of respect of his children, and Gloria's cold indifference annoys him. She is equally cool with Valentine, who tries to convince her he, too, is concerned with women's rights. Failing, he berates her as a prig, disconcerts her by claiming there is a chemical attraction between them, and kisses her. Gloria, shamed and disturbed, complains to her mother of this lack in her education.

In the Clandons' hotel sitting room Mrs. Clandon is correcting proofs. She learns from the twins of Gloria's and Valentine's attachment, and when she tries to convince Valentine (and herself) that Gloria, as a modern educated woman, is immune, he says he has technically trained himself to conquer that type of woman in the sex duel. Gloria resents her mother's interference and despises her own weakness, but icily rejects Valentine. M'Comas informs them that Crampton is demanding custody of the under-age twins and tries in vain to persuade Mrs. Clandon to a reconciliation.

During a ball at the hotel that night, M'Comas and Crampton come to the room to meet Bohun, Q.C., who is the waiter's son. Gloria and her father have a partial reconciliation, and Bohun decisively concludes that Crampton has no case: only a friendly arrangement is possible. Valentine and Gloria settle their disputes and become engaged, and Bohun waltzes off with the bride-to-be to the ball, into which all the family are swept.

THE DEVIL'S DISCIPLE (1897)

They call me the Devil's Disciple . . .

The year is 1777, the time of the American War of Independence. Mrs. Dudgeon, a puritanical, self-righteous woman, learns that her husband has died and that his brother Peter, whose illegitimate daughter Essie lives with her on bare sufferance, has been hanged in a nearby town by the British troops as a rebel. Her son Richard, a renegade in her eyes, also supports the American colonies. Pastor Anthony Anderson tells her that her husband at the last minute changed his will in favour of his rebel son. The Dudgeon relatives come to the house for the reading of the will and Dick lightheartedly mocks them. The will leaves him his father's house and property, and his first gesture is to befriend the cowed girl Essie, to the indignation of Pastor Anderson's pretty young wife Judith, who is both shocked and attracted by Dick.

At the Andersons' house, Anderson tells the frightened Judith of rumours that Major Swindon, of the British Army, intends to hang one of the town's rebels as an example: he believes this will be Dick. Dick comes to the house and Anderson warns him of his danger. Dick believes the danger is to Anderson himself. The Pastor will not listen. He is called away to Dick's mother, who is ill, leaving Judith reluctantly to give tea to Dick. The English soldiers arrive to arrest Anderson, and Dick, deliberately putting on Anderson's coat, allows them to take him away. He warns Judith to find Anderson and get him out of harm's way, and she swoons as he kisses her goodbye. When Anderson comes back he learns what has happened and is transformed into a man of action. He rides off with pistols, apparently to save himself but telling Judith to get word to Dick to 'hold his tongue until morning'.

At the British headquarters in the Town Hall Dick is to be tried as Anthony Anderson. Judith bribes a Sergeant to allow her to speak to him, saying she is his wife. She tells Dick that Anderson has run away. Dick says that is just what he wanted, and cannot convince her that his attitude is practical, not heroic, and that he did not act for her sake as she obviously hopes. She disconcerts him by admitting she loves him but promises to keep quiet at the trial. This is conducted by Major Swindon and General Burgoyne, a witty, civilised commander who covers his distaste for the business with irony and is bitterly aware that Springtown is already in the hands of the rebels. He and Dudgeon appreciate each other, but Judith, at sentence of death, breaks her promise and desperately reveals that Dick is not really Anderson. Nevertheless, as Dick had warned Judith, Swindon still decides to hang him as an example. Burgoyne, who has retired with dispatches, returns and reveals to Swindon that he has had a demand to surrender the town from the rebels who have taken Springtown, and that he is forced to do so because, owing to a War Office blunder, the expected reinforcements will not reach him.

At the gallows Dick is about to be hanged when Anderson rides up. He brings a safe-conduct from Springtown, accepts Burgoyne's surrender and demands Dick's immediate release. The crisis has revealed to the Pastor his true nature and vocation, and he is now a captain in the Springtown militia. Dick promises Judith not to tell her husband of her confession.

Caesar and Cleopatra (1898)

> *In the little world yonder, Sphinx, my place is as high as yours in this great desert; only I wander, and you sit still; I conquer, and you endure . . .*

Caesar is alone at night in the desert, soliloquising to the Sphinx. He is startled by a young girl hiding in its paws. It is Cleopatra, frightened of the Romans who she says are coming to eat them all. She reveals she is the Queen, but driven from the throne by her young brother Ptolemy. Caesar, not disclosing his identity, says she must tonight meet Caesar in her palace, and if he thinks her worthy to rule, he will make her the real ruler of Egypt. She takes him to the palace throne room and he encourages her to give orders and act as Queen, in spite of the protests of her formidable nurse, Ftatateeta. Cleopatra is exultant in her new-found tyrannical power, but still terrified of the invader's coming. Caesar commands her to meet Caesar alone. He sits beside her throne. The Roman soldiers hail him as they enter, and Cleopatra, realising who he is, falls with relief into his arms.

In Alexandria Caesar confronts the child king Ptolemy and his advisers and demands taxes, as a conqueror. He sends for Cleopatra who drags her brother from the throne, but Caesar returns him to it, and proposes they shall rule jointly. There is some rebelliousness among the Egyptians, and Caesar is not, as they expected, pleased to find they have murdered his Roman opponent, Pompey. He advises Ptolemy to follow his friends and guardian, Pothinus, who have left the palace. Cleopatra is threatening to throw Ftatateeta to the crocodiles and says to the shocked Caesar, 'if you do as I tell you, you will soon learn to govern'. He forces her to submit to his judgment and humours her interest in the younger Mark Antony. Pothinus brings an ultimatum from the Egyptians, who are raising an army and burning the harbour. Cleopatra helps Caesar into his armour and he goes out to seize the lighthouse, having diverted the Egyptians to try to save the burning Alexandria Library.

On the quay, Apollodorus, a young Sicilian merchant, has brought carpets for Cleopatra. Cleopatra comes down and Apollodorus offers to row her to the lighthouse, but the Romans fight him to prevent it. Apollodorus then proposes to take a present from Cleopatra to Caesar, and says he will give her, for the present, the richest of his carpets. Later the rolled carpet is brought from the palace by Ftatateeta, carefully carried by porters, and rowed away with Apollodorus in the boat.

The carpet is brought to Caesar at the lighthouse, and raised with Apollodorus by crane. When it is unrolled Cleopatra steps out, and is tearful to find herself viewed as an encumbrance. As the boat has sunk they are cut off, but Apollodorus dives into the sea to swim to the Roman galleys, and Caesar follows. The terrified Cleopatra is thrown after him, and he swims away with her on his back.

A year later (47 B.C.) Cleopatra is in her boudoir with her ladies and musicians. Pothinus has bribed Ftatateeta to let him see her. He finds Cleopatra no longer a child or easily hoodwinked, and believes she is betraying Egypt for Caesar's sake. Caesar comes in for a feast on the roof garden. Pothinus is granted audience and charges that Cleopatra is hoping to reign alone in Egypt and get rid of Caesar, if necessary by killing him. Caesar says it is only natural and lets Pothinus go. Cleopatra whispers to Ftatateeta that he must not leave the palace alive, and later a cry is heard. There is the roar of an angry multitude, and Caesar realises from her fear and cajolery that Cleopatra is hiding something serious. He learns the populace are angry at the murder of Pothinus. When Cleopatra admits he was slain by her order, Caesar threatens to leave her to the mob. He learns that relief is arriving for the Romans and leaves for battle. Rufio, his loyal soldier, realises that Ftatateeta was Pothinus's assassin, and after he has left she is found on the altar of Ra with her throat cut.

In the last scene, Caesar takes leave of Cleopatra, and learns from her mourning garment of Ftatateeta's murder. Rufio admits he killed her, but Caesar refuses Cleopatra's plea for vengeance. However, as he sails away, he promises to send her Mark Antony.

CAPTAIN BRASSBOUND'S CONVERSION (1899)

I claim as a notable merit in the authorship of this play that I have been intelligent enough to steal its scenery, its surroundings, its atmosphere, its geography, its knowledge of the east . . . from an excellent book of philosophic travel and vivid adventure entitled 'Mogreb-el-Acksa' (Morocco the Most Holy) by Cunninghame Graham.

A Scots missionary, Rankin, living on the heights overlooking the harbour of Mogador, is visited by two English tourists, Sir Howard Hallam and his charming sister-in-law, Lady Cecily Waynflete. Rankin reminds Hallam, a retired eminent lawyer, that they have met before, when Hallam's brother Miles sailed for Brazil. Hallam says his brother died 30 years ago, leaving a property in the West Indies, which was illegally taken over by an agent. Owing to cost the matter was not contested until years later, when Hallam went out there, found the estate being handled by another agent and persuaded the man to hand it over to him. Owing to the collapse of the sugar industry it was now running at a loss.

Lady Cecily proposes a trip into the Atlas Mountains, and Captain Brassbound, a local trader, is suggested as escort. Brassbound, a handsome, dark, saturnine man of 36, recalls to Rankin his old friend Miles Hallam. Brassbound only reluctantly agrees to provide the escort, which turns out to comprise mostly British ex-criminals and ne'er-do-well aristocrats. Lady Cecily shows she has no fear of them and intends to look after them, but Brassbound warns Hallam that the 'justice of the hills is the justice of vengeance'.

The scene shifts to a Moorish castle in the hills. One of Brassbound's men, Marzo, is wounded in a skirmish and Lady Cecily nurses him and effectively takes control of the whole escort. Brassbound declares that Hallam is his prisoner, but that he is not a brigand seeking ransom, but his nephew, seeking revenge. His mother, Miles's wife, a Brazilian, had appealed to Hallam in vain to claim the estate for her and been driven to drink and madness when he refused. She had threatened to kill him and been sent to prison by Hallam. Later, after her death, Hallam had claimed the estate himself. Hallam protests that he did not know of a son: he was then a struggling barrister, not the Attorney-General he later became. Brassbound says he must appeal to the Sheikh Sidi el Assif, the local law-giver (who hates Christians), for whom he has sent. Hallam says Brassbound can have the property if he claims it, but Brassbound says he will not sell his mother's revenge for ten properties, while Lady Cecily, as placid as ever, mildly points out that the property is losing money in any case and not worth having.

Brassbound orders Hallam to be taken away, and is non-plussed to find Lady Cecily mending his coat. She infuriates him by saying he is like his uncle, with a dogged temper, ruling by force. He tells her she is in danger but she remains equable. The Sheikh is in sight and Brassbound warns her he has made a bargain with him to escort only Jews and believers, not Christians. He brought them here for revenge. However, when he hears that the Sheikh's overlord, the Cadi of Kintafi, is also on his way he decides to let the Sheikh in and try to hold him in talk until the Cadi arrives to protect them.

When Sidi arrives Lady Cecily herself disarms him. He offers to let Brassbound keep Hallam in exchange for the woman, to which Lady Cecily, to everyone's horror, pleasantly agrees. The Cadi now arrives, in fear of British and American reprisals, and orders Brassbound, his men and the Sheikh to be seized. Hamlin Kearney, captain of the American cruiser *Santiago*, holds an enquiry at which Lady Cecily gives evidence for Hallam, in such a way that she exonerates Brassbound from blame. Afterwards, they meet and he tears up the souvenirs of his revenge, including his mother's photograph. He confesses that his life has lost direction. He proposes marriage, and Lady Cecily is almost mesmerised by him into accepting. But gunfire from his ship, the *Thanksgiving*, rescues them: he is drawn back to his ship while she cries 'What an escape!'

THE ADMIRABLE BASHVILLE; or CONSTANCY UNREWARDED (1901)

Shaw's novel, *Cashel Byron's Profession*, was dramatised by him in blank verse. Lydia Carew, the owner of Wiltstoken Castle, is lamenting her loneliness when Cashel Byron meets her. He is disturbed to discover her social position and cannot bring himself to tell her he is a prizefighter. His trainer, Mellish, fears he will lose his forthcoming fight, and Cashel knocks him down for his pessimism; but when Bashville, Lydia's footman, subsequently reads her a report of the fight it is to the effect that Cashel has won.

Having discovered Cashel's identity, Lydia refuses to see him when he calls and Bashville goes out and knocks him down. This moves Lydia to admit Cashel, who says that his mother had been an actress, hence his Shakespearean manner of speech. She is impressed, but begs him to change his profession: he refuses. Lydia goes to fetch her hat to accompany Cashel to another fight. Bashville strikes Cashel again, and the latter reflects that the footman is cut out to be a boxer himself. At the Islington Agricultural Hall, the Zulu chief Cetewayo reveals his contempt of fisticuffs as a way of fighting, and he and his followers run amok as Cashel and his opponent begin the contest. Cashel beats back the Zulus and rescues Lydia, who faints on seeing that he is injured. At Wiltstoken the police break up a prizefight involving Cashel. He appeals to Lydia for shelter, but she refuses at first, relenting afterwards and lying to the police. Cashel's mother, Adelaide, comes looking for him, lamenting like a tragedy queen that he had left her ten years before to become a prize-fighter. He rejects her. When the police arrest him, Adelaide discloses that Cashel is the son of the high-born Sieur of Park Lane and Overlord of Dorset. A message arrives from the Throne giving Cashel full amnesty and the rank of Deputy-Lieutenant of Dorset. Lord Worthington, his backer, proposes to Adelaide and is accepted. Bashville, who had had pretensions towards Lydia, relinquishes her to Cashel and agrees to take up boxing under the name 'the Admirable Bashville, Byron's Novice'.

MAN AND SUPERMAN (1903)

> *Not yet created! Then my work is not yet done . . .*
> *A father! a father for the Superman!*

John Tanner, young rebellious author of *The Revolutionist's Handbook and Pocket Companion*, is furious and alarmed to discover that under the will of the late Mr. Whitefield he is made a guardian of his daughter, Ann, jointly with Roebuck Ramsden, a lawyer friend of the family who violently disapproves of Tanner. Tanner, unlike Ramsden and Whitefield's adopted son Octavius (Tavy) Robinson, is aware that Ann gets her own way in everything by hypocritically saying it is her parents' wish. He believes she has designs on Octavius, who is idyllically in love with her. Ann, as he expects, meekly supports her father's will. Everyone (except Tanner) is concerned to discover that Tavy's sister Violet, who is unmarried, has been seen visiting a doctor wearing a wedding ring. Tanner proclaims her courage in fulfilling her true woman's function and defying society. Violet, however, proves obstinate about being packed off abroad, and when Tanner congratulates her is as outraged as the others have been at her supposed immorality. She quells them all by confessing she is married, but has reason to keep her marriage a secret.

Shortly afterwards Tanner's chauffeur Henry Straker, an independent, mechanical-minded product of the Polytechnic, is jealous when Tanner tells him the steam car of an American, Hector Malone, has raced them to Richmond. He whistles a tune sceptically when Tanner says that Ann's young sister Rhoda is to ride in their car while Ann goes with Tavy in the American car. Tavy reports he has proposed to Ann and been repulsed, ·on the grounds that he should have consulted her guardian, Jack. Tanner is sure this is one of Ann's tricks and warns Tavy the trap is closing on him. He receives a note from Rhoda saying Ann has forbidden her to go out alone with him. Almost immediately Ann comes out and says Rhoda cannot come because she is ill. Faced with her lie, she puts the blame on her mother. Tanner harangues her about independence and rhetorically tells her to break her chains and come for a fast ride with him to Marseilles and across to Morocco. To his horror and alarm, she takes this literally and agrees to come. Her mother says she meant to ask Tanner to take Rhoda out sometime too. To cover this *gaffe* Ann introduces Hector Malone, the young American, who proposes that Violet shall go in his car and appears thunderstruck when warned she is a married woman; but when the others have left he kisses Violet. He is her husband and it is clear it is she who demands secrecy. This is because Malone's father, a wealthy manufacturer, will disinherit him if he does not marry an English title.

Tanner, left alone with Straker, demands the reason he always whistles at mention of Ann. Straker tells him Ann has no intention of marrying Tavy: it is Tanner she is interested in. Tanner, greatly alarmed, tells Straker to break the speed record to Biskra and they flee in the car.

Act III is an Interlude usually omitted but sometimes performed separately under the title *Don Juan in Hell*. In the Sierra Nevada, Mendoza, an educated brigand chief, discusses politics with his followers while waiting to hold up motor cars 'and secure a more equitable distribution of wealth'. They capture Tanner and Straker, and after Tanner's agreeing to a ransom Mendoza confesses that unrequited love drove him to banditry. His love turns out to be Straker's sister Louisa. Tanner and he fall asleep as Mendoza reads his love poetry. Some Mozartian music is heard as Tanner dreams. He has become Don Juan Tenorio, his ancestor. He tells a wandering old woman, just dead, that she is in Hell and she is highly indignant, especially when Don Juan tells her he killed the father of a woman who screamed at his advances. She says her own father died in just such a duel. Juan, deeply bored with Hell, tells her she can here be any age, and she becomes young and very like Ann Whitefield. Juan recognises her as Doña Ana, the lady of the duel. The D minor chord and its dominant announce the Statue of Anna's father, now on pleasant terms with Don Juan. He is like Roebuck Ramsden. The Devil (Mendoza) joins them, nauseating Juan with his aesthetic romanticisms. He tells Doña Ana anyone can go to Heaven but most find it intolerably dull. Juan longs for Heaven to spend his aeons in contemplation, or the work of helping Life in its struggle upward. But the Devil maintains Man has used his superior brain only to create engines of destruction: 'the power that governs the earth is not the Power of Life, but the power of Death'. Juan retorts that Man's cowardice can be overcome by ideas. Man will overcome fear if fighting for a purpose. And he must 'make himself something more than a mere instrument of woman's purpose'. He chooses Heaven and goes to it, while the Devil reflects on the Superman idea that Juan is pursuing. To Ana's query, 'Where can I find the Superman?' he answers that the Superman is not yet created. Ana goes to seek a father for the Superman, and the vision of Hell vanishes.

Tanner wakes up and the motoring party of Ann, Violet, Hector, Tavy, and Ramsden join them. Soldiers also arrive to arrest the brigands, but Tanner saves them by saying they are his escort.

In Act IV (usually played as Act III in the theatre), the party has reached Granada. In a villa garden an Irish-American, Hector's father, confronts Violet Robinson. He has intercepted a note addressed by her to his son and states that if Hector marries her he will disinherit him. Violet is dealing with this in her cool, reasoning way when Hector comes in prepared to quarrel with his father. To the astonishment of Tanner and the others he announces he will marry Violet if he pleases. Tanner puts his foot in it by saying he knows Violet is married already; and the truth that the man is Hector is forced out. Hector proclaims he won't take the old man's money in any case and leaves his father pleading with Violet to win him round. When they have all gone, Ann tells Tavy her mother insists on her marrying Jack, and adds she would only make Tavy unhappy: she could not live up to his ideal. Jack has no illusions about her. Her mother denies to Jack that she influenced Ann to marry him but makes it clear she thinks it would serve Ann right, as he alone could master her. Jack, left with Ann, explosively refuses to marry her although everyone, as he says, seems to regard it as settled. He feels himself in the grip of the Life Force but has still not yielded when he seizes her in his arms. Ann promptly faints and everyone rushes back. She comes to only when it is certain Tanner has yielded, and he launches into an apostrophe on their loss of happiness and freedom.

JOHN BULL's OTHER ISLAND (1904)

> *An Irishman's imagination never lets him alone . . .*
> *If you want to interest him in Ireland youve got to*

*call the unfortunate island Kathleen ni Hoolihan
and pretend shes a little old woman. It saves thinking.*

Laurence Doyle and Thomas Broadbent, both bachelors,
are partners in civil engineering. Broadbent, an Englishman, proposes to go to Ireland to form a Land Development Syndicate but Doyle, an Irishman, is depressed at
Broadbent's sentimentality about the Irish and Home Rule.
He also fears to return there because Nora Reilly, who has
a 'fortune' of £40 a year in Roscullen, seems to have
preserved an attachment to him which he wishes to avoid;
but Broadbent's interest in Nora rouses his hopes.

In Roscullen, Father Keegan, an eccentric and imaginative ex-priest, believed to be mad, converses about
Ireland with a grasshopper. He is joined by Nora Reilly
who is pleased to hear that he believes travelled men return
in the end to country girls at home. Broadbent, who has
arrived ahead of Larry, goes to the Round Tower to look
for Nora, who is disappointed it is not Larry. Broadbent
is enchanted by her, but Nora recognises that he has had
too much of the local poteen.

Next morning Broadbent tells Larry he proposed to
Nora and wonders about his obligation. A deputation,
including the local priest, Father Dempsey, proposes that
Larry shall replace their present M.P. as he knows the land
problems, but they are outraged when he suggests he
would, in that case, agitate for their labourer Patsy
Farrell to get a wage rise to £1 a week, and other
reforms. Broadbent is more anxious for the seat and im-
presses the deputation.

Nora is upset to realise Larry's indifference. Broadbent
finds her in tears, comforts her and again proposes. She
finds herself, without delight, used as electioneering bait
and introduced to all and sundry as the future M.P.'s
wife. Larry assures her she has done well for herself, and he

and Broadbent go ahead with plans to build a hotel and golf links, and make money at the expense of the Irish.

How He Lied to Her Husband (1904)

In a flat in the Cromwell Road a youth in elegant evening dress is romantically waiting for the married woman who occupies the flat. She arrives flustered, having lost the youth's love poems, and says that owing to her unusual name of Aurora she will be easily identified as the woman to whom they are addressed. She disillusions the poet by her fear of her sisters-in-law and refusal to leave her husband on the spot. Her husband returns with the poems, given him by his sister, and is unexpectedly indignant when the poet pretends they were not written to his wife. He takes the poet's indifference as a slight on his wife. The men fight, are separated by the wife, and are reconciled. The husband asks if he can have the poems printed and the disillusioned author of them suggests as title, 'How He Lied to Her Husband'.

Major Barbara (1905)

> *It is cheap work converting starving men with a Bible in one hand and a slice of bread in the other. I will undertake to convert West Ham to Maho-metanism on the same terms. Try your hand on my men: their souls are hungry because their bodies are full.*

Lady Britomart Undershaft is worried about the future of her daughter Barbara, who has joined the Salvation Army and intends to marry Adolphus Cusins, a Professor of Greek of limited means. Her other daughter, Sarah, will also need financial support as her fiancé, Charles Lomax, cannot inherit his wealth until he is 35. She feels that her husband Andrew, a rich armaments manufacturer, should give them more money. She tells her son Stephen that she separated from Undershaft, who was a foundling, because he wished to disinherit Stephen for an adopted foundling, following a long tradition of the firm. She has invited him to the house. Undershaft arrives and meets them all, including the two girls and their fiancés. He agrees to come to Barbara's West Ham Salvation Army Shelter if she will visit his armaments factory the following day.

At the Shelter there are the usual flotsam seeking food; a layabout with anti-capitalist ideas, 'Snobby' Price, who pretends to be a mother-beater 'saved' by the Army; an old woman, Rummy Mitchens, who pretends to be a 'saved' prostitute; and Peter Shirley, a genuine unemployed man near starvation, unable to get work because he is grey-haired. A rough, Bill Walker, comes in and threatens and strikes the young Army worker, Jenny Hill, because she has taken his girl from him. Shirley stands up to him and says he only hits women and starving men but wouldn't face his relative Todger Fairmile, who stood up to professional wrestlers at the music hall. Barbara also worries his conscience by her placid emphasis on his striking Jenny. She says his girl has moved to another shelter and got herself another man, Todger Fairmile; and Shirley dares him to go and tackle him. Bill, shamed but angered by Barbara's nagging, eventually goes off to get his face bashed in by Todger, telling Cusins he'll be worn out if he marries Barbara. Cusins suspects he is right but says it will be worth it. Undershaft visits the Shelter and maintains his creed of money and gunpowder, without which salvation and the graces of life are unattainable; and he warns Cusins that Barbara will soon see through his banging of a Salvation Army drum, which is a mere pretence to be near her. The two men like each other, but Cusins doubts Undershaft's assertion that he can buy the Salvation Army and thus pass on to Barbara, who has the character to inherit it, his armaments empire. Barbara refuses her father's offer of even twopence to supplement her collection, saying it is money badly earned. Bill Walker returns dusty, Todger having knelt on, and prayed over, him. He offers a sovereign to Barbara as conscience salve, and Undershaft offers to make it up to a hundred. Barbara refuses; but the Salvation Army Commissioner, Mrs. Baines, arrives and accepts £5,000 from Undershaft, who offers it to force Lord Saxmunden (Bodger of Bodger's whisky) to pay his promised £1,000. Cusins ironically rejoices and leads the band, with Undershaft, to the Assembly Hall meeting. But Bill Walker proves to be a cynical lost convert and Barbara, disillusioned, takes off her badge.

At home, Lady Britomart discusses the question of the cannon inheritance with Undershaft who is delighted to find that Stephen, in any case, prefers to go into politics. The whole family gathers and goes to the armaments factory. A town has been built for the workers, who enjoy the best social benefits. This ensures their loyalty and Undershaft's rising profits. Lady Britomart demands that she have a share in running the town and proposes that Undershaft shall appoint Cusins, Barbara's intended husband, as his successor. The foundling difficulty is settled with casuistry when Cusins admits that his mother and father, though married in Australia, are not legally married in England, as his father married his deceased wife's sister (forbidden in English law at the time of the play, 1905). Cusins immediately asserts his power by beating up Undershaft's salary offer. Barbara remains disillusioned, until her father points out that poverty is the world's greatest crime. In the Army shelter it enabled her to win men's souls by the bribe of bread, but here she will have more success: 'their souls are hungry because their bodies are full'. To Cusins he points out: 'Whatever can blow men up can blow society up'. Dare he make war on war? Cusins decides for the factory, not knowing if he will thereby lose Barbara. But Barbara too feels she can use the power of this place for spiritual good. As Cusins says, 'the way of life lies through the factory of death'.

PASSION, POISON, AND PETRIFACTION; or, THE FATAL GAZOGENE (1905)

Lady Magnesia, in bed, is approached by her husband Fitztollemache, with a dagger. She sneezes; he collapses in shock and tries to explain away the dagger. He is jealous of Augustus, who comes to show off his new suit, half black, half yellow, with a spangled waistcoat. The husband poisons the drink in the gazogene, and Augustus writhes in agony and hears a heavenly choir singing 'Won't you come home, Bill Bailey'. Fitztollemache repents and suggests lime as an antidote, and they force Augustus to eat the ceiling plaster. He is petrified; a policeman, landlord and doctor are killed by lightning ('The copper attracted the lightning'); and Magnesia and Fitztollemache have them swept into the corner, and erect, and pay homage to, the living monument of Augustus. The Angels sing 'Bill Bailey'.

THE DOCTOR'S DILEMMA (1906)

> *It's not an easy case to judge, is it? Blenkinsop's an honest decent man; but is he any use? Dubedat's a rotten blackguard; but he's a genuine source of pretty and pleasant and good things.*

Dr. Ridgeon has been knighted in the Honours List and is now Sir Colenso Ridgeon. Sir Patrick Cullen, a veteran doctor, and others come to congratulate him. Sir Patrick maintains that no medical 'discovery' is new, not even Ridgeon's cure for consumption by inoculation. Ridgeon explains that he is now able to 'time' the inoculation so as to make a cure certain; but, wrongly timed, the serum can kill. The effusive Cutler Walpole, much addicted to fashionable surgery and removing the 'nuciform sac', joins them, as does Sir Ralph Bloomfield Bonington, known as 'B.B.', a royal physician of beaming self-satisfaction. He startles Ridgeon by saying he has borrowed his new serum and used it on little Prince Henry, and this has resulted in Ridgeon's knighthood. A shabby general practitioner, Dr. Blenkinsop, who knew Ridgeon at medical school, also calls.

A beautiful woman, Mrs. Dubedat, who has been trying in vain to see Ridgeon, has, he learns, already spoken to some of the doctors downstairs and when they go he is persuaded to see her. She says her husband is consumptive and pleads with Ridgeon to save him. Ridgeon explains that his hospital and staff have already the limit of chosen cases under treatment, but she urges that her husband is a great artist and shows Ridgeon some of his sketches, which impress him. Ridgeon is still troubled by the thought of sacrificing one of the patients under treatment and compromises by inviting Mrs. Dubedat and her husband to the party to celebrate his knighthood. There Dubedat will meet all the other eminent doctors and he will abide by their decision.

At the Star and Garter, Richmond, after dinner, Mrs. Dubedat is assured by the doctors that they have been charmed by Louis and he is worth saving. After they have gone it emerges that Louis has borrowed money from most of them. Moreover the hotel maid, Minnie, asks for his address and says she is his wife. They had spent her savings on honeymoon and then she had to return to service and has not seen him since. Ridgeon learns that the worthy Dr. Blenkinsop has tuberculosis, and he and Sir Patrick discuss the dilemma of the choice between him and Louis. Ridgeon can take only one for his cure: he points out that if he lets Blenkinsop die; no one can accuse him of doing it to marry his widow. He is confident Jennifer Dubedat would marry him if Louis died. He could, the two men decide, 'not strive officiously to keep alive' by leaving Dubedat in the hands of 'B.B.'.

Dubedat is painting Jennifer in his studio. They expect the doctors to call, and when Ridgeon comes Louis tries to borrow £150 from him, suggesting a scheme by which Ridgeon can get it back by blackmailing Jennifer. Dubedat appears to have no moral feelings about this, and airily suggests also that Ridgeon could blackmail his rich patients into buying his pictures. Taxed with his marriage to Minnie Tinwell he coolly asks if they are sure he is 'married' to Jennifer. He taunts them with their 'morality' and says they would wreck Jennifer's life and Minnie's if they reported the bigamy. They realise he is right but all decline to treat him, except 'B.B.'.

Several months later Louis is dying, 'B.B.' having mistimed the treatment and killed instead of cured. Louis has begged Jennifer to let him die in the studio. He asks her not to mourn for him but to help him to immortality, giving the world her beauty in place of the pictures he did not live to paint. He dies stating the creed to which he has been faithful—the creed of the artist who believes in Michelangelo, Rembrandt, the might of design and the mystery of colour, and never having betrayed his artist's principles by lowering his standards to make money. The body is taken out; Jennifer returns radiantly dressed as he had asked her.

A year later, at Louis' one-man show, Ridgeon sees Jennifer again. She is amazed to learn that he, 'an old man' (he is 50), could care for her, and, piqued, he admits he allowed Dubedat to be killed. She still idealises the artist, but has remarried, as Louis desired. Staggered, Ridgeon exclaims, 'Then I have committed a purely disinterested murder!'

GETTING MARRIED (1908)

> *I wonder who will begin the stand against marriage. It must come some day.*

In the Palace of the Bishop of Chelsea the Bishop's lady, Mrs. Bridgenorth, is discussing the wedding of her daughter Edith to Cecil Sykes with William Collins, the greengrocer, who is in charge of the arrangements. He tells her his brother George is married to a highly susceptible woman who has left him for other men several times. He always takes her back, and her experiences have made her much more interesting than a stay-at-home wife. Mrs. Bridgenorth's brother-in-law, General Bridgenorth, arrives and also her sister Lesbia Grantham, who is 'not a marrying woman' and who rejected the still-disconsolate General 20 years before. She says she is too fastidious and independent to have a man about the house, and none could equal her romantic dreams. She would make a good mother, but as society declares she cannot have children without putting up with a man, the country must do without her children.

Bridgenorth's eldest brother Reginald arrives. His much younger wife, Leo, has just divorced him, but when she arrives she greets Reginald with friendliness, and it transpires the divorce was 'arranged' so that she could marry St. John Hotchkiss. The Bishop, a tolerant man, is receiving love letters from an unknown woman who confesses to other lovers but wants an idealized relationship with him in heaven. Edith has locked herself in her room reading a pamphlet on marriage, and the Bishop says that owing to our refusal to change our divorce laws, England, like ancient Rome, will soon give up marriage as an institution.

St. John Hotchkiss, an elegant young self-avowed snob, arrives to report that the bridegroom, Cecil, has also locked himself in his room, declaring that he was not aware, when proposing, of what he was letting himself in for legally. He now hestitates to marry Edith, a reforming, outspoken young woman who may make him responsible for her libels. Edith too has discovered that she will never be able to get a divorce if Cecil becomes a murderer or thief or otherwise impossible as a husband. Hotchkiss and others propose drawing up a new kind of partnership deed, and Collins is appealed to. He suggests that Mrs. George, the Mayoress and coal merchant's wife, would give admirable advice.

Mrs. George is summoned and recognises Hotchkiss, who explains to the men that he had, when very young, gone to complain about her husband's coals and fallen in love with her. Now the attraction has revived and he must flee. Mrs. George proposes instead that he gives up Leo and comes to visit home and amuse her husband. If he succeeds, he may try to win her own burnt-out affection. He tries to trap her by force into instant yielding, and the Bishop comes in as she threatens him with the poker. She bursts into tears and alone with the Bishop confesses she is the woman of the letters. Later, she falls into a trance, speaking mystically of the love she gives men and her small return. Hotchkiss comes in and helps wake her. Then the others return and Edith says she has been married to Cecil by the beadle. They have been to an insurance agency to insure Cecil against her libels. Leo proposes to return to Reginald who needs looking after; Hotchkiss proclaims his preference for Mrs. George; Lesbia rejoices that she is still 'a glorious strong-minded old maid of old England'; while Hotchkiss makes it clear to Mrs. George that she has nothing to fear, since once in her home he will be unable to betray her husband because of his honourable instincts.

THE SHEWING-UP OF BLANCO POSNET (1909)

Anyhow, I got the rotten feel off me for a minute of my life; and I'll go through fire to get it off me again.

To a barn-like Court Room in the Wild West, Elder Daniels brings Blanco Posnet, accused of stealing the Sheriff's horse, which he denies. He derides everyone and says he left the town at sunrise because it is a rotten town, and that the horse presumably did the same, for the same reason: if he had taken the horse he would have been riding it and they would not have caught up with him.

When Blanco is left with Elder Daniels it transpires he is Daniels's brother and traded the horse because he thought it was his, since Daniels owed him money and had taken everything when their parents died. He is exasperated by Daniels's preaching and hypocrisy and talks mysteriously of a woman and child whom he believes were not real, but sent by God to trick him into being hanged, out of spite for the godless life he has led. A vindictive prostitute, Feemy Evans, is brought in to witness that she saw Blanco on the horse, but he maintains that she had been too drunk to see anything. The jury is prejudiced by Blanco's mockery and Sheriff Kemp has to prevent their dragging him out to be hanged. The proceedings are interrupted by another woman who has been caught in possession of the horse. She says she took it to get her dying child to a doctor; the dead baby is outside. She denies that Blanco was the man who gave her the horse, and Feemy, unnerved by talk of the dead child, goes back on her identification. The Sheriff rules that it is no theft to commandeer a horse to get a dying child to a doctor and forces the Court's spectators, who resent being deprived of a hanging, to take up a collection for the mother. Blanco launches into a sermon on the mixed nature of good and evil, and shakes hands with Feemy who had been touched by the good, too.

PRESS CUTTINGS (1909)

A woman suffragette has chained herself outside the War Office, and General Mitchener has a message from the Prime Minister asking him to free her (key enclosed) and see her. When brought in 'she' divests herself of garments and turns out to be the Prime Minister, Balsquith. It is the only way he can get in through the suffragettes outside. They discuss the strategy of dispersing the suffragettes and countering possible German invasion. They are joined by the President (Lady Corinthia Fanshawe) and Secretary (Mrs. Banger) of the Anti-Suffragette League. Mrs. Banger intimidates General Sandstone, who proposes to her. She becomes virtually head of the army. Lady Corinthia, failing to captivate Mitchener, marries the Prime Minister. General Mitchener in relief proposes to the Irish charlady, Mrs. Farrell, and is accepted.

THE FASCINATING FOUNDLING (1909)

The Lord Chancellor (Guardian of Wards in Chancery) is visited by Brabazon, a young man foundling, who wishes him to find him a place on the stage, and also a wife; and by Anastasia Vulliamy, a young woman foundling (left on a doorstep in Park Lane, which gives her social status) searching for a husband. Brabazon returns and she falls into his arms. Hearing she has no money he is reluctant, but when she explains that she is also a foundling and will bring no relations to pester him, he agrees to marry her.

THE GLIMPSE OF REALITY (1909)

A 'tragedietta' set in fifteenth-century Italy.

Count Ferruccio, a young, ruthless nobleman, disguised as an old friar, hears the confession of a young girl that she is to lure him to his death. His enemies will pay the reward to her father, the innkeeper, Squarcio, and she will have the dowry to wed the fisherman Sandro. He throws off his disguise and alternately threatens them and argues with them for his life. He even offers marriage to the girl, Giulia, who has noble blood. She has no pity, as the rich have none for the poor they oppress, and in facing terror Ferruccio discovers his soul; not in the religious sense, but in recognition that he has been spoilt from babyhood with dreams of power, and now faces reality for the first time. The would-be murderers now believe him a little mad. Since the mad come under the protection of God and the Saints, they spare him, and he arranges a bright future for Giulia.

Misalliance (1910)

What do I tell Johnny when he brags about Tarleton's Underwear? It's not the underwear. The underwear be hanged! Anybody can make underwear. Anybody can sell underwear. Tarleton's Ideas: that's whats done it.

Johnny Tarleton, son of a self-made wealthy manufacturer of underwear, John Tarleton, is irritated by his sister Hypatia's fiancé, the young, aristocratic Bentley Summerhays, who has brains but physical timidity. Bentley's father, Lord Summerhays, tends to agree, but it transpires he has himself asked Hypatia to marry him and been rejected. Hypatia is attracted by Bentley's brains but not romantically. Tarleton, her father, who is always quoting literature, is something of a lady's man. Hypatia is bored by her parents and elders, and when an aeroplane makes a forced landing in the garden falls in love with its pilot, Joey Percival, a friend of Bentley. The men, including Tarleton senior, are all attracted by his passenger, a Polish acrobat named Lina Szczepanowska, who is a strong character fully determined to keep her independence and proud of her ability to earn her own living. A young man intruder sees Hypatia chasing Percival. He proves to be a natural son of Tarleton, bent on avenging his mother by shooting Tarleton. Lina disarms him by strength, and Mrs. Tarleton by sympathy. Hypatia revolts her father by asking him to buy Percival for her: Percival says he cannot afford to marry her otherwise. Tarleton reluctantly agrees, but the gaps between the generations, and parents and children (the theme of the play), are emphasised.

The Dark Lady of the Sonnets (1910)

A man (Will Shakespear) is challenged by a beefeater as he goes to visit a dark lady. He says he gave her four tickets to the Globe Theatre with which to bribe the warder, and offers him in addition a writing-tablet as a free pass. The beefeater complains that he cannot understand these new fangled plays, but he accepts gold to see *The Spanish Tragedy* and upsets Will by saying the dark lady, Mary Fitton, has to bribe him to admit her friends, including Shakespear's friend Lord Pembroke. Will, however, adds to his tablets several sayings of the warder for later use in his plays, and does the same when a veiled lady, whom he at first takes to be his Mary, sleepwalks into the garden wringing her hands and saying that all the perfumes of Arabia cannot whiten her Tudor hand. When she wakes, Shakespear rhapsodises on her musical sense of words and expresses love for her. The Dark Lady, finding them there, jealously cuffs them apart; and the other lady unveils and cries 'High treason!' The Dark Lady cries she is lost, she has struck the Queen, but Will only protests in capitals, 'Woman! You have struck WILLIAM SHAKESPEAR!!!!' He is outraged when the Queen takes him for a servant and slights his family. He throws doubts on her own legitimacy, but as she is about to strike him he dextrously turns a line into a compliment on her looks. The Dark Lady is allowed to go, and Shakespear, pressing his advantage with Elizabeth, asks a boon: the endowment of a National Theatre, which he says is desperately needed to stage his own best plays, and those of others, which cannot catch the ears of the groundlings like his *As You Like It* and *Much Ado About Nothing*. Elizabeth says sadly it will be 300 years before her subjects learn that man cannot live by bread alone, 'but by every word that cometh from the mouth of those whom God inspires'. Shakespear begs her prayers for his theatre and Elizabeth says that is her prayer to posterity.

(Written in 1910 to support the agitation for a National Theatre.)

FANNY'S FIRST PLAY (1911)

> *These things really do happen to real people every day; and you read about them in the papers and think its all right ... And really I'd rather go out and assault another policeman and go back to Holloway than keep talking round and round it like this.*

A wealthy aesthete, the Count O'Dowda, is preparing to stage privately a play by his daughter, whom he believes to share his eighteenth-century tastes. The daughter, Fanny, has, however, been to Cambridge, and confesses to Trotter, one of four critics invited to the play, that the work may distress her father as it is a modern one. The critics do not know who wrote it.

Fanny's play begins. Mr. and Mrs. Gilbey have had a letter about the disgraceful behaviour of their son, Bobby. They have no idea what this behaviour is, as he has disappeared. They are visited by a Miss Dora Delaney, a flamboyant but kindly young woman of dubious way of life, who describes a night out in which both she and Bobby were arrested as drunk and disorderly. She has served a two-week sentence but Bobby is in prison for a month and she wishes them to raise his bail. Mr. Gilbey is angry at her leading his son astray but goes off to Wormwood Scrubs to release him.

That afternoon Mr. and Mrs. Knox, whose daughter Margaret is Bobby's fiancée, are worrying why the Gilbeys have dropped them. They imagine they must have found out that Margaret has run away. Margaret now returns with a young Frenchman, Lieutenant Duvallet, whom the Knoxes imagine is the man she ran away with. She says, however, she has been in Holloway Gaol for assaulting a policeman. She and Duvallet both resisted police attacks in a theatre on Boat Race night and she is determined to tell everyone. The Knoxes' only wish has been to keep it dark, for fear of the disgrace.

Margaret arrives at the Gilbeys' and makes Bobby admit that their engagement was their parents' doing and that they really feel more like brother and sister. They soon learn that each has been in prison. Dora enters and recognises Margaret as Prisoner No. 406. Margaret is annoyed at Bobby's snobbish attitude about her knowing a girl like Dora and they come to blows. Juggins the footman shows in Duvallet, and, warned of the approach of Mr. and Mrs. Gilbey, the young people all go into Juggins' pantry for tea.

Juggins gives a month's notice to Mr. Gilbey. It transpires he is younger brother to a duke, who is ill and now needs him. The Knoxes call and discuss with the Gilbeys the curious attraction Margaret and Bobby have for people since they were in prison: respectability seems unnecessary after all. They hear the party downstairs and ask the young people to come up. Duvallet, taxed about his intentions towards Margaret, protests he is married with two daughters and wants an English education for them, for

only here can women escape quite respectably from family
tyranny. Juggins says Bobby should marry Dora; it is the
gentlemanly thing to do and they both enjoy a non-
respectable type of living. He himself is willing to marry
Margaret who has already expressed interest in him.

In the Epilogue the Count is duly horrified by the play
and its offence against Art, and the four critics all disagree
about its merits and who wrote it, but unite in the opinion
that it could not be by Shaw (who only writes about himself, etc.). Fanny is distressed by their criticism, but on
finding that she wrote it they delight her by saying they
thought it was by Granville Barker or Pinero. Trotter
realises the prison experience was her own—she recently
served a month as a suffragette. All now combine to
applaud the actors.

ANDROCLES AND THE LION (1912)

> *I really dont think I could consent to go to heaven*
> *if I thought there were to be no animals there.*

In Roman times, a lion with a wounded paw is befriended
by a hen-pecked Christian tailor, Androcles, who extracts
a thorn from its paw after his wife has fled in terror. The
grateful lion and Androcles waltz off together.

Some Christian prisoners are brought to Rome, and a
handsome young Captain engages in argument with the
Christian girl Lavinia. The Captain points out they can
save themselves by sacrificing to the gods. Lavinia answers
that their faith makes life wonderful so it is not easy to die,
but their faith must meet the test. The Captain is troubled
in conscience and attracted by Lavinia. He warns the
Centurion to expect three more prisoners, among them a
dangerous armourer named Ferrovius, and Lavinia asks if
this is the Ferrovius who has made wonderful conversions

in the northern cities. The Captain says he has 'the strength of an elephant and the temper of a mad bull'. Ferrovius, Androcles and Spintho are brought in. Androcles has been arrested as a sorcerer: he made a pet of the 10th Army's leopard. Ferrovius with a heroic effort turns the other cheek when struck by a Roman. He has a great fear: that when brought into the arena he will forget his Christian meekness and thrash the gladiator. The craven thief Spintho is embracing martyrdom only in the hope of eternal life.

Behind scenes at the Coliseum, Spintho takes fright, offers to sacrifice and dashes into a passage, where a lion being prepared for the arena eats him. Now a new, hungry lion has to be found for the Christians. The Emperor passes and is struck by Ferrovius's physique. He offers him a post in the Praetorian Guards if he can defeat his gladiator, but Ferrovius refuses to fight. He and the men go into the arena, leaving Androcles and the women, who are to go to the lions together. The Captain again urges Lavinia to save herself and offers marriage, but she asks him if he would wish his son to be a coward. A man is sent into the arena to attack Ferrovius, who with other Christians is refusing to fight. Ferrovius, incensed, slays him and six gladiators. He is in an agony of shame, but the Emperor is delighted: it is a new record. He proclaims that the persecution of the Christians shall cease: they are all free. The menagerie keeper begs one Christian for the new lion or the people will riot, and Androcles is sent into the arena. The lion proves to be the one of the wounded paw and they have an ecstatic reunion. The Emperor is chased by the lion and Androcles begs him to pretend he is Androcles's friend. This quiets the lion. Ferrovius realises his true nature and accepts a place in the Praetorian Guard. Lavinia remains Christian but says the Captain may visit her sometimes. Androcles and his lion are allowed to go in peace.

OVERRULED (1912)

A young lady and gentleman, Gregory Lunn and Mrs. Juno are flirting but learn that each is married. Nevertheless, they find that enjoyment outweighs respectability. They are interrupted by the approaching voices of their respective spouses, and retire into dark corners as these enter. The scene is approximately repeated between the new pair, on the same chesterfield. Eventually both couples confront each other, and the husbands and wives admit mutual devotion but also pleasure in the company of the other pair. One husband has a slight guilt complex, and the other begins to get confused as to which of the ladies he is actually married to. The ladies take it all sensibly and see no reason to forgo the company of their admirer. Eventually they go in to dinner, each lady escorted by the other's husband.

PYGMALION (1913)

> *You see this creature with her kerbstone English: the English that will keep her in the gutter to the end of her days. Well, sir, in three months I could pass that girl off as a duchess at an ambassador's garden party. I could even get her a place as lady's maid or shop assistant, which requires better English.*

In the rain at Covent Garden after an opera performance, Professor Henry Higgins meets Colonel Pickering, author of *Spoken Sanscrit*, and bets him that he could pass off the Covent Garden flower girl, Eliza Doolittle, as a duchess within three months, if he were to practise on her his knowledge of phonetics. He tosses the outraged girl a handful of money and goes off to dinner with the Colonel. She is delighted to find florins and sovereigns, and promptly orders a taxi home.

Next day Eliza calls at Higgins's laboratory in Wimpole Street and grandly asks for lessons in speech, to enable her to work in a flower shop. She offers payment at 1s. a week. Higgins bullies her but is attracted by the idea of transforming her. Pickering bets him the expenses of the experiment if he can pass her off as a duchess at an ambassador's garden party, and Higgins orders his housekeeper, to Eliza's shrill protest, to bathe and reclothe her. Eliza suspects Higgins's intentions but in the end reluctantly agrees to the experiment. Higgins is then visited by Eliza's father, Alfred Doolittle, a dustman, who demands his daughter and is taken aback when Higgins tells him to take her. Higgins, interested in his sense of rhetoric, finally gives Doolittle £5 and the dustman leaves, failing to recognise his clean and transformed daughter on the way out.

Some months later, at the house of Higgins's mother, Higgins proposes to introduce Eliza to her guests. These include the Eynsford Hills, a mother, daughter, and son, Freddy, who is immensely taken with what he considers Eliza's fashionable 'small talk' in an exquisite high-class accent, but she commits some Cockney solecisms, including the celebrated 'Not bloody likely.' Only Mrs. Higgins is troubled about the girl's future, and her son's and Pickering's attitude to their 'doll'.

Back at Higgins's house, late one night, Eliza, gorgeously dressed, returns with Higgins and Pickering from her greatest test, a garden party, dinner party and the opera. She has won Higgins his wager but he is bored with the experiment, and he and Pickering, congratulating themselves, ignore her. In a helpless rage she throws Higgins's slippers at him, but he cannot comprehend her feelings, and when she asks what is to become of her suggests she may marry someone. She asks if the clothes are hers, as she doesn't want to be accused of stealing when she goes. She hands back the hired jewellery to

Higgins, who is indignant at what he considers her ingratitude.

Next morning Higgins visits his mother in a state because Eliza has 'bolted'. He is followed by Eliza's father, now affluent and unhappy owing to a legacy from a friend of Higgins who took seriously Higgins's joke about Doolittle being the 'most original moralist' in England. Mrs. Higgins says Eliza is upstairs and rebukes her son and Pickering for their inconsiderate treatment of her. When Eliza comes down she tells Pickering it was from his manners she learned to be a lady, and threatens Higgins that she will go as assistant to his rival, Professor Nepean, and teach him Higgins's methods. Higgins is furious but at the same time begins to admire her, and assumes she will return to Wimpole Street. Eliza, who is being wooed by Freddy, is not so sure.

GREAT CATHERINE (1913)

Patiomkin (as Shaw spells Potemkin), 'the ablest man in Russia', ex-lover and present minister of Catherine II, is working in the Winter Palace, St. Petersburg, 1776. An English captain, Edstaston of the Light Dragoons, comes asking for an audience with the Empress. He has served against the rebels in the American War of Independence and has been instructed to describe the events of the war to her. Patiomkin, a huge, drunken, untidy man, suggests that Edstaston hopes to win the Queen's favour and is knocked down by the Captain. When the guard are called, Edstaston coolly draws his pistols. Patiomkin orders them out and sends for diamonds for his attacker, who refuses them. Patiomkin is amazed and impressed, and advises the flabbergasted and indignant Englishman against attempting to become Tsar when (inevitably) he has become Catherine's lover. He and his pretty niece drag Edstaston protesting to Catherine's bedchamber.

The Empress, in bed, awakes, attended by her Court. Patiomkin literally carries the protesting Edstaston into her presence and dumps him on her bed, to her wrath and secret amusement. Edstaston naively shows admiration for Catherine, who leaves to be dressed. When Patiomkin claims to have made his fortune, Edstaston protests that he is engaged to be married and his fiancée is in St. Petersburg. When Catherine orders him to come to her he rushes out to join his fiancée, Claire, in a garden by the Neva. Here he is seized and after a fight carried off by Catherine's soldiers. Claire bribes a sergeant to get her into the palace, where Edstaston is brought, trussed, before Catherine who demands to be left alone with him. She proceeds to read a pamphlet by Voltaire and maddens Edstaston by tickling him when he shows an English officer's contempt for radical philosophy. Claire hears his cries, breaks in and loosens his bonds, belabouring Catherine who exercises iron self-control. Edstaston talks them out of the palace with a spate of puritanical English advice to Catherine that leaves the Empress and Patiomkin speechless. Catherine wishes she could have had him, not as a lover, but for her museum.

THE MUSIC-CURE (1913)

Reginald Fitzambey, a young official at the War Office is having a nervous breakdown, with his doctor trying to calm him. He distractedly maintains that he meant no harm in buying up macaroni shares on learning that the Army was to be put on a vegetarian diet, but the Opposition is making capital out of it and he has been interrogated by a Committee. The doctor suggests a music-cure and gives him opium pills. As he sleeps a lady enters, plays the piano and wakes him. She says she is Strega Thundridge, known as 'the female Paderewski', and has been given a large fee by his mother the Duchess, to play for two hours. Reginald, who dreads people, is horrified to learn that crowds have gathered on the stairs and outside the house to listen to her, and that he will be forced to endure classical music. He is, however, transported by Chopin's Polonaise in A Flat and confesses that he longs for a strong, splendid, beautiful woman to cling to. Strega discloses to him a dream of a timid, gentle husband whom she would probably beat but cherish. They play the wedding march together.

O'FLAHERTY, V.C. (1915)

Private Dennis O'Flaherty has won the Victoria Cross in World War I. It is 1915 and he is about to be fêted in his native Ireland. He startles the local baronet, General Sir Pearce Madegan, with a new questioning spirit about the war and its necessity, and the information that Madegan's employee, O'Flaherty's mother, has always secretly been pro-Irish and a Catholic totally opposed to the English. When she arrives for tea she berates O'Flaherty, having believed he was fighting against the English, not for them; while the servant girl Teresa, for whom O'Flaherty has brought back a gold chain, casts only a mercenary eye on the possibility of his pension. Mrs. O'Flaherty has *her* eye on the girl's 'fortune' of £10, but O'Flaherty has seen through her and proclaims his intention of marrying a French wife. Teresa and Mrs. O'Flaherty quarrel violently over the gold chain, and O'Flaherty tells Sir Pearce that at the front he had actually longed for a peaceful hour at home. 'Some likes war's alarums; and some likes home life. I've tried both, sir; and I'm all for war's alarums now.' And Sir Pearce replies: ' . . . as one soldier to another, do you think we should have got an army without conscription if domestic life had been as happy as people say it is?'

THE INCA OF PERUSALEM (1916)

An Archdeacon, Daffodil Donkin, protests to his daughter Ermyntrude that he cannot maintain her in her extravagance. He had married her off to a millionaire, now dead, whose assets have proved illusory, partly owing to the war. He suggests she had better become lady's maid to a princess until she can find another millionaire to marry her.

A helpless and nervous spinster princess, without a maid owing to the war, engages Ermyntrude, who immediately takes strong action against waiter and hotel manager and acquires the best suite. The Princess confides that she is to be married, against her will, to one of the sons of the Inca of Perusalem, who has never seen her. The Inca is coming to decide which son will best suit her. Ermyntrude receives him, pretending to be the princess, while he pretends to be a Captain Duval. He boasts of his artistic capabilities, and proposes that Ermyntrude shall marry him, even though she rejects his present of jewellery as in vulgar taste. She points out he is impoverished by the war, like all monarchs, and advises him to capitulate to his enemies, as young men will go on dying until he does. He protests that people seem to prefer war to art. Both admit that they know the other's identity and in the end they go out for a drive and tea at the zoo.

AUGUSTUS DOES HIS BIT (1916)

Lord Augustus Highcastle has been recruiting without effect in Little Pifflington and finds only one 57-year-old clerk remaining as the entire Town Hall staff (even he is called up before the end of the play). A beautiful woman calls and says her sister-in-law, a German, has made a bet with Highcastle's brother at the War Office that she will obtain the secret list of gun emplacements in Augustus's possession. As Augustus argues with the clerk she extracts the list from its envelope and replaces it with a blank sheet of paper. She makes her excuses and leaves, but from the street calls up to the clerk to witness that she got away with the list. She then makes Augustus connect her with his brother on the telephone and tells the brother the story. Augustus is consoled by the thought that the laugh at his expense will cheer the lads on leave from the trenches.

ANNAJANSKA, THE BOLSHEVIK EMPRESS (1917)

'A revolutionary romancelet'. General Strammfest, hereditarily devoted to the Panjandrina of Beotia, is horrified to learn that the Princess Annajanska has deserted to the Revolutionaries. Brought to him a prisoner, she defends her action and says the varied revolutionary factions fighting for power are no crueller than the rulers of her family have been. She despises the General for his slavish sentimental attachment to the royal family and reveals under her furs the uniform of the Hussars. She proposes to unite the revolutionary factions as the Bolshevik Empress.

HEARTBREAK HOUSE (1919)

A Fantasia in the Russian Manner on English themes.
> . . . *this silly house, this strangely happy house, this agonizing house, this house without foundations. I shall call it Heartbreak House.*

The house shared by old Captain Shotover with his daughter Hesione and her husband has quarters fashioned like the poop of a ship. A young girl, Ellie Dunn, has been invited by Hesione to stay but no one has remembered. The eighty-six-year-old Captain takes a fancy to her and fusses over her in his eccentric way. He is by no means as rambling mentally as he seems, though rough of tongue about his other daughter, Lady Utterword (Ariadne), whom he imagines to be in the outer reaches of the Empire. Lady Utterword, however, also turns up after 23 years and finds the house equally unprepared for her. She is upset that the Captain refuses to recognise her. He reiterates that he is striving to attain the seventh degree of concentration. When Hesione Hushabye, the elder daughter and a beauty, comes in she explains that Ellie is to marry Mangan, a 'perfect hog' of a millionaire, for the sake of her father, Mazzini Dunn, who is poor. It transpires that Mangan lent Ellie's father capital to start a business and when the money was gone, and her father bankrupt, took over the business, made it thrive and appointed her father manager. Hesione is intrigued to find the girl romanticising about Othello and Desdemona, and comparing Othello's adventures with those of a handsome stranger she met and who told her fabulous stories. Hesione's scepticism is justified when her husband, Hector, comes in and Ellie recognises him as the Marcus Darnley of her tale. The revelation hardens and embitters Ellie but Hesione tells her that in spite of his lies Hector really has won medals for bravery, and if his courage is questioned he will instantly do something really dangerous. Mangan, Ellie's father and Lady Utterword's brother-in-law, Randall, arrive. Randall is apparently enamoured of Lady Utterword; and Hector himself is attracted, talking of the 'strange fascination of the daughters of that supernatural old man'. Lady Utterword warns him she is strictly conventional, but agrees to flirtation 'in play'. The Captain now attempts to live by his inventions and has a store of explosive in the gravel pit in the garden 'to blow up the human race if it goes too far'. He starts on a new invention at Hesione's request, as household funds have run low.

After dinner Mangan tells Ellie he ruined her father on purpose, so he could reap the financial benefit of the busi-

ness. Ellie still wishes to keep to her bargain and marry
him, although Mangan admits he is in love with Hesione.
She blackmails him by telling him she will see that he
never enters Hesione's house again if he refuses to marry
her. Disillusioned by Hector, she looks on marriage now
only as a financial undertaking. Mangan, rather outraged,
complains of a headache and she sends him into a hypnotic
sleep by massaging his forehead. The others find him, and
Ellie's father says Ellie did the same to him long ago. He
is distressed by Hesione's pointing out Mangan's un-
suitability for Ellie but thinks Ellie is actually the stronger
character. Hesione tackles Ellie and finds she is determined
on the marriage: it is her only escape from poverty. When
Ellie awakens Mangan he is furious and upset at the things
he has heard them say, in his trance. A crash and a shot are
heard from upstairs. A burglar is caught, but when he
assures them that he will get ten years they decide not to
call the police, and find themselves bribing him to go
without trouble. The burglar is recognised by Captain
Shotover as his old reprobate ship's mate, Dunn, whom he
has been confusing throughout the play with Ellie's father.
He is also the husband of the servant, Nurse Guinness.
Hesione takes Mangan out into the garden and the Captain
and Ellie are left alone, musing on life, the need for riches,
and the soul. When they, too, go into the garden there is a
scene between Hector (resplendent in Arabian clothes) and
Randall about Ariadne, and Hector is left crying 'Women!'
in exasperation.

In the garden it is night; the couples wander together
and discuss the strange quality of the house and its effect
on them. Lady Utterword says it lacks horses and there
are only two classes in good English society, the equestrian
classes and the neurotic classes. Mangan confesses he has
no money for use: he lives on travelling expenses and com-
mission. The factories belong to the shareholders, who pay
for him to represent them in the Government. He is

indignant when Ellie says she never really intended to marry him: she is spiritually married to Captain Shotover. She names the house Heartbreak House, and the Captain says England is like a ship which will strike the rocks and sink unless they learn navigation. An explosion is heard: it is a bombing raid. The burglar flees for shelter to the gravel pit, where Mangan is already hiding. The others hear a tremendous explosion, as the gravel pit, with its store of explosives, is destroyed. They listen to the departure of the aeroplanes as Randall plays his flute.

BACK TO METHUSELAH (1920)

Part I: In the Beginning

Imagination is the beginning of creation.

In the Garden of Eden, Adam discovers a fawn which has stumbled and broken its neck. He and Eve realise it is dead, and, for the first time, that death must eventually come to them. They are horrified at the thought of one of them being left alone, but Adam is depressed also by the tedious prospect of eternal life. While he is burying the fawn, the Serpent wakes and asks Eve to admire her new hood. She has learnt to speak by listening to them, and says she is the subtlest and wisest of creatures. She tells Eve that death can be overcome by birth. She herself casts her skin and renews herself, but in addition there is 'a second birth', which she achieved by taking a part of her body, encasing it in white and exposing it to the sun until a little snake came out. Eve says she does not trust the sun but longs for a way to save Adam from perishing. The Serpent tells her of Lilith who tore herself asunder to give birth to Adam and Eve, because two must share the burden of creation: the labour is too terrible for one. She conceived by imagination and will. Adam cannot do this, for if

Lilith had made him so he could do without Eve. Eve cannot create without Adam, however, and the means is a great secret. Adam is pleased by the prospect of handing on the burden of weeding to another gardener, but Eve fears that if there are other Adams and Eves he may kill her. Adam says there is a Voice against killing and something binds them together. The Serpent gives them another new word, 'love'. Adam, laughing his first laugh, leaves the Serpent and the woman 'to whisper secrets', and Eve recoils as the Serpent whispers in her ear.

A few centuries later, in an oasis in Mesopotamia, Adam is digging and Eve spinning. Cain enters in warlike attire and taunts Adam with his lack of progress and ideas. Adam accuses him of murdering his brother. But Cain dreams of great armies of men destroying each other, and wants his mother to create them for this purpose. Eve maintains he risks his life and kills the animals and birds only to provide furs and food for his good-for-nothing wife, her daughter Lua. To Cain's claim that he is something higher than man, hero and superman, she says he is simply Anti-Man. He taunts his parents as simple country folk and says why not bring men and women up from childhood to slave for them and think of them as gods. Adam is tempted but Eve indignant. She asks why, if the Voice warned Adam not to kill, it did not also warn Cain. Cain retorts that it did, but he was not afraid of the Voice. He hears another Voice, promising life after death, and despises Adam's Voice which he calls the Devil, because it chains him to digging and to the earth. He wants something higher and nobler. Eve also speaks of hope of better things, suggested by the children who do not dig or fight but tell 'beautiful lies in beautiful words', 'cut reeds of different lengths and blow through them, making lovely patterns of sound in the air', or 'make little mammoths out of clay'. Nevertheless she is troubled, for 'death is gaining on life', and already their grandchildren die before they have learned how to live. But man need not live by bread alone. There is something else. They do not yet know what it is; but when they find out there will be no more digging, spinning, fighting or killing.

Part II: The Gospel of the Brothers Barnabas

Creative Evolution doesnt stop while people are laughing.

Soon after World War I two brothers, Franklyn and Conrad Barnabas, an ex-cleric and a biologist, discuss their theory of Creative Evolution. They have come to the conclusion that for the fuller development of man's maturity and achievement it is necessary for him to live at least three hundred years, and that, if the idea is planted in people's minds, nature, which proceeds by occasional evolutionary 'jumps', will subconsciously work on their imagination and will, and this end will be achieved. They are joined by Franklyn's daughter 'Savvy' (short for 'Savage'), a modern young woman of the 'twenties, and her admirer, the young local rector, Bill Haslam, who is a charming nitwit with small vocation for the Church. The parlor maid says she and the cook have read the Conrads' book about longevity. She is about to get married and confesses that if she were faced with a life of several centuries she would hesitate to tie herself.

The brothers are visited by two Liberal Party leaders, Joyce Burge and Henry Hopkins Lubin, who are under the impression they have a scheme helpful to winning the General Election. Their political humbug is satirised, and when it appears the brothers have no concrete 'elixir' they lose interest, although fertile in ideas for political exploitation of the theory. Haslam and Savvy are also lightheartedly sceptical, especially when told the first evolutionary leap into long life might be made by anyone, even the parlor maid: the first man or woman to live three hundred years may not have the slightest notion that he is going to do it, and may laugh at the idea louder than anyone. 'Well, it wont be one of us, anyhow,' says Haslam, to which Franklyn has the unanswerable reply, 'How do you know?'

Part III: The Thing Happens

Consider my situation when I first made the amazing discovery that I was destined to live three hundred years!

The scene is the official parlour of the President of the British Islands, 2170 A.D. Burge-Lubin, the President (a descendant of the two politicians of the previous play), is on the television-telephone to Barnabas, his Accountant General, and with difficulty persuades him to go to a cinema show to be given to a visiting American who has invented a system for breathing under water. Burge-Lubin wishes to play marine golf and contacts the Minister of Health, a Negress, with whom he is having a flirtation by television-telephone. He has little official work as affairs of state are virtually run by the Chief Secretary, a wise Chinaman named Confucius.

Burge-Lubin and Confucius are disturbed by Barnabas, who agitatedly reports that the films shown to the American—of high officials whose lives were shortened by drowning during the past few centuries—has revealed that four of them, a President, a General, and two Archbishops, are one and the same person as the present Archbishop of York. This prelate is announced and proves to be Bill Haslam, now very authoritative and apparently some forty-five years of age. He admits he is two hundred and eighty-three years old, and because of pension and other difficulties created by his unique survival he has been forced to stage several 'deaths' and start life again elsewhere. He had no idea he was to become a long-liver until his wife, Savvy Barnabas, died at sixty-eight and commented on his curious youthfulness. His hearers do not at first believe his tale, but when they are joined by the Domestic Minister, Mrs. Lutestring, she and the Archbishop have a feeling that they have met before. It transpires she was once the Barnabas's parlor maid. She is now two hundred and seventy-four. They realise it is in their power to multiply long-livers who may inherit their accumulated wisdom, and go off to discuss marriage. The others, over-awed by their personalities, now believe their story but find themselves powerless to interfere with them, much as they fear them, because they themselves may prove to be longlivers without yet knowing it. Confucius realises there are certainly other long-livers, and the Archbishop will now attempt to find and organise them.

Part IV: Tragedy of an Elderly Gentleman.

How often must I tell you that we are made wise not by the recollections of our past, but by the responsibilities of our future.

The scene is Burrin pier, Galway Bay, Ireland, 3,000 A.D.

An Elderly Gentleman, from the capital of the British Commonwealth, Baghdad, is on a sentimental pilgrimage to the islands of his ancestors, and is distressed to find it impossible to make his colloquial British language and morals understood. He is warned by an inhabitant, the long-liver Fusima, that it is dangerous for short-livers to come here, owing to a disease, discouragement. Fusima leaves him in charge of a male nurse, Zozim, who explains that Fusima is a secondary (i.e. in her second century) and sends for a companion for him nearer his own age, Zoo, a young girl of 56. She tells him he cannot be understood because thoughts die sooner than languages, but the oracles will understand him. He says he has not come to consult the oracles but is travelling for pleasure with his daughter, his son-in-law the British Prime Minister, and General Aufsteig, who is really the Emperor of Turania, 'the greatest military genius of the age'. Zoo shocks him by her long-liver's views but she claims the superiority of the long-lived, because they look to the future, not the past. When he tries to escape she tunes in to a higher authority and he is stayed by an electric shock. He scolds her and arouses in her an instinct to kill him, as she says the long-livers kill evil children, and she is so shattered by this self-discovery that she now believes all short-livers should be exterminated and the long-livers should conquer the world. She adds that the Prime Minister only pretends to wish guidance from the oracle; in fact he comes simply to boast of the added authority the visit gives him. The oracle's actual words are always twisted to suit visiting politicians' own wishes. She leads the Elderly Gentleman to the temple.

Outside the temple a short man, very like Napoleon Bonaparte, confronts a veiled woman, the oracle, with the announcement that he is the Man of Destiny. She is un-impressed and says he must await the prescribed ritual. As he shows contempt for the ritual, she agrees he may consult her now, but warns him she is veiled with insulating material because without it he could not endure her presence. As he challenges this, she unveils and he quails with terror. When she re-veils, he tries to pass it off. He makes clear he is a military genius whose talent is to inspire men to kill each other. Only as a slayer can he become a ruler, for he has no talent except to organise war.

But in time even the victors demand the fruits of victory, and if he goes on making war he will be dethroned. How is he to escape the dilemma? The oracle warns him that warriors are not popular in these sacred islands, and he draws a pistol. She forces him to part with it by threatening to unveil, and then tells him the answer to his problem: 'to die before the tide of glory turns'. She shoots him and he falls, but rises after she leaves with a diatribe ending: 'And missed me at five yards! Thats a woman all over.'

Zoo arrives with the Elderly Gentleman, the British Envoy and his wife and daughter. Napoleon is immobilised off-stage by an electric current. Zoo says she and Zozim must dress up for the ritual to impress them: they themselves don't believe in it but the tourists expect it. After talk with Zozim the Elderly Gentleman again becomes greatly discouraged.

In the temple, the Oracle (or Pythoness) receives the party who are terrified by the trick effects. The Envoy recovers by swallowing half a pint of neat brandy and after an incomprehensible political oration eventually gets to his point: whether the government should face an election in August or put it off till the spring. The Elderly Gentleman adds that 15 years ago another Prime Minister came to consult the Oracle and the Oracle prophesied that his party would be victorious. The Envoy demands to be answered exactly as his illustrious predecessor was, upon which the Oracle says 'Go home, poor fool.' Zoo says it is the same reply their predecessor got. The Envoy decides to tell his countrymen the exact truth: that the Oracle repeated to him, word for word, what it said to Sir Fuller Eastwind 15 years ago. The Elderly Gentleman, left alone, implores the Pythoness for guidance, saying he cannot in conscience connive at this chicanery. He begs to be allowed to' stay. She compassionately offers him her hands, he grasps them, looks at her face, and falls dead. 'Poor short-lived thing! What else could I do for you?' she says.

Part V: As Far as Thought Can Reach

Nothing remains beautiful and interesting except thought, because the thought is the life.

The scene is a sunlit glade outside a temple, 31,920 A.D. 'Children' are dancing, playing and making love: children in this era being born at 18 years old and moving into adolescence four years later, when maturing minds press them on to more satisfying activities than the arts and pleasure. A girl, Chloe, who has lied about her age to her boy-friend, Strephon (who is only two, half her age), has just reached this point of development and wants now only to wander in the woods and think about mathematics. Strephon, a romantic, is desolate.

The He-Ancient intrudes on the players, walking in a dream of thought. He is 800 years old; bald and almost without clothes. He is kindly and indulgent towards the 'children', who are horrified at his ascetic way of life; but he tells them that 'one moment of the ecstasy of life as we live it would strike you dead'. He advises them to let the Ancients enjoy themselves in their own fashion.

Acis, a youth of almost three, comes from the temple and reminds them that today there is to be a birth and a Festival of the Arts. The baby is kicking at its shell and vociferously demanding to be born. A She-Ancient arrives to act as midwife. She breaks the shell of the giant egg and a baby girl, Amaryllis, is born, washed and clothed. She looks about 17 years old, makes babyish, delighted discoveries about life and attaches herself passionately to Strephon, who is still moping for Chloe. The She-Ancient instructs her that she will live indefinitely but in the end be destroyed by an accident: this is inevitable, and must happen to the She-Ancient herself. She leaves the children to their Festival.

They are revolted to find that a sculptor, Arjillax, has made statues like the Ancients, instead of the beautiful ones

of young people they are used to. He defends his work as
creative art, showing the growth of maturity. A girl-
critic, Ecrasia, resents this, saying the business of the
artist is to create beauty. Arjillax's master, Martellus, is
criticised for not creating anything at all: he is moving into
adolescence, and has smashed all his statues because he cannot give them life. He has, however, modelled two life-
size ones for the scientist Pygmalion, who tells them he has
at last succeeded in infusing them with life. He brings out
the man-made Man and Woman, who revolt everyone
with automaton-like reflexes. They are examples of 'pre-
historic man' of thousands of years before. The Woman
bites the hand of Pygmalion, her creator, who falls dead.
She and the Man are terrified of the result and accuse each
other. They die of discouragement and are destroyed at
order of the two Ancients, who warn the children of the
dangers of making such 'dolls'. The He-Ancient tells Acis
he can really create nothing but himself. The She-Ancient
explains 'art is the magic mirror you make to reflect your
invisible dreams in visible pictures'; but the Ancients do
not need mirrors or works of art; they have 'a direct sense
of life'. Yet they too have troubles, the body which will
inevitably be destroyed, 'the last doll to be discarded'. The
body ties them to death, and their destiny, to be immortal,
is not achieved. 'The day will come when there will be no
people, only thought'.

Darkness comes and the ghosts of Adam and Eve, Cain
and the Serpent appear. They are replaced by Lilith, the
mother of creation, who 'brought life into the whirlpool of
force'. She ends the play with a great soliloquy on the
development of mankind, whom she is always about to destroy as a failure, and supersede with a new and better form
of life; but until now she has always stayed her hand, because they have made a leap forward like this one of
creative evolution and long life. She gave to Eve the
greatest of gifts, curiosity, and still has that herself, and

patience. 'I can wait: waiting and patience mean nothing to the eternal.' 'Let them dread, of all things, stagnation; for from the moment I, Lilith, lose hope and faith in them, they are doomed . . . Of Life only is there no end; and though of its million starry mansions many are empty and many still unbuilt . . . my seed shall one day fill it and master its matter to its uttermost confines. And for what may be beyond, the eyesight of Lilith is too short. It is enough that there is a beyond.'

JITTA'S ATONEMENT (1922)

This play was a translation and adaptation by Shaw of the play of the same name by the Austrian dramatist, Siegfried Trebitsch.

SAINT JOAN (1923)

> *Must then a Christ perish in torment in every age to save those that have no imagination?*

In Vaucouleurs, 1429 A.D., the hens have ceased to lay, and the Captain of the castle, Robert de Baudricourt, is furious with his steward when he says it is an Act of God because de Baudricourt has refused to see the girl from Domrémy, Joan of Arc. De Baudricourt sends for Joan who meets him brightly confident. She demands a horse, armour and soldiers to go to the Dauphin and raise the siege of Orleans, saying it is the will of God. Three of the men have promised to go with her, and de Baudricourt is amazed to find they include the squire Bertrand de Poulengey. De Poulengey manages to convince de Baudricourt that the girl's faith might put heart into the soldiers and he agrees to let them go. When they have gone, the steward rushes in to say the hens are laying like mad, and de Baudricourt gasps, 'She did come from God.'

At Chinon, in Touraine, Charles, the Dauphin, is bullied by his court, including the Archbishop of Rheims. Only Charles has any faith in Joan's mission but when she is announced agrees to hide and let Gilles de Rais, a courtier, take his place on the throne, to test Joan's ability to identify him. On entering, her soldier's clothes and short hair cause merriment but she immediately recognises de Rais by his blue beard, and finds and kneels to the Dauphin. Charles takes this as miraculous and the worldly Archbishop, although he sees the rational explanation, is shamed by Joan's reverence for himself. Against some opposition she succeeds in getting command of the army and permission to try to raise the siege.

On 29 April, 1429, Dunois, known as 'the Bastard', a young commander of the army, is frustratedly waiting for a change of wind so that he can cross the River Loire and raise the siege of Orleans. He is joined by Joan, who is impatient of his delay until he explains the cause. Almost immediately afterwards the wind changes.

Some time later, in a tent in the English camp, Joan's enemies discuss how they can destroy her. They are the Earl of Warwick, who represents the English nobility and feudal system, the Bishop of Beauvais, representing the Roman Catholic Church, and de Stogumber, an English chaplain of unimaginative conventional patriotism and virulence towards Joan. All see Joan as a supreme danger to the systems they represent, although both the Bishop and Warwick, a political opportunist, are without personal malice towards her. The Bishop, in fact, disturbs Warwick by refusing to guarantee that if she is captured she will automatically be condemned by the Church and handed over to the secular arm for execution. It is the duty of the Church to save the girl's soul by extracting confession and repentance if possible. They agree, however, to sink their differences.

In the Cathedral at Rheims the Dauphin has just been

crowned King. Joan agrees when Dunois, her only real friend, says she is a little in love with war. She asks naïvely why the courtiers hate her, and Dunois points out that stupid people never love those who show them up and supersede them. When the Dauphin and Archbishop come in there is a discussion on the need to continue the war and take Paris—Joan's view—or to seize the opportunity for a treaty: and Dunois points out luck will not always be on their side. The Earl of Warwick has offered £16,000 for Joan's capture, and the day she is dragged from her horse and imprisoned, and no miracle intervenes to save her, her life will not be worth the life of one of his soldiers. Joan agrees this is true if God lets her be beaten, but is discouraged to find no one present thinks her worth the ransom, and that the English threaten to burn her as a witch. Nevertheless she clings to her faith in her 'voices', to the anger of the Archbishop who says she is setting herself above the Church. She recognises in the end that she stands alone, and that her loneliness is her strength, as it is God's strength.

In Rouen, on 30 May, 1429, Joan is brought before the Bishop of Beauvais' court to be tried for heresy. The Inquisition is represented by the Inquisitor, who before Joan appears explains the disastrous consequences of heresy to the Church and society, but suggests that Joan herself is basically innocent for she has no idea of the significance of what she has done. He entreats the court to act with mercy and justice and ignore the purely temporal charges with which de Stogumber and others are clouding the main issue.

Joan is brought in in chains and shows the strain of long imprisonment and trial. But she withstands questioning with hardy commonsense, unaware that through her attitude she is condemning herself for heresy, for she puts her own judgment, inspired by her 'voices', before that of the Church. A young monk, Brother Ladvenu, tries sympathetically to make her see this, and instances the fact that her voices told her to wear soldiers' clothes as proof that they come, not from God, but the Devil. She retorts that it is entirely practical advice for a woman surrounded by soldiers: dressed as a man, they think of her as a man. She is, though, shaken when at last she realises the executioner present is prepared to burn her as a witch that day, and Ladvenu presses home the point that her 'voices', who had promised to save her, had lied. She agrees to recant, but on finding that this means, not release, but perpetual imprisonment, tears up the recantation. She knows now her 'voices' were right: the counsel of the court is of the Devil, and hers of God.

She is solemnly excommunicated and taken away. Warwick stays away from the fire and de Stogumber stumbles back from it in mental torment, appalled by the cruelty he had been too unimaginative to envisage. The executioner comes in and reports that there are no relics, as Warwick commanded: 'You have seen the last of her.' 'The last of her?' says Warwick reflectively. 'Hm! I wonder!'

The Epilogue takes place in June, 1456. Charles VII, formerly the Dauphin, is in bed. The courts have reconsidered Joan's case and rehabilitated her, and Brother Ladvenu comes to tell the news to the King. It is a wild, blustery night and Charles, left alone, dreams or imagines he is visited by Joan and the ghosts of the men who knew or condemned her: some still living, some dead. All now praise her. A strange figure from the future, 1920, also appears and announces her canonisation. She proposes now she is rehabilitated to return to earth, and is saddened that at this even her truest friends, like Dunois, hesitate and flee. A white radiance descends on her as she cries: 'O God that madest this beautiful earth, when will it be ready to receive Thy saints? How long, O Lord, how long?'

THE APPLE CART (1929)

> *Ministers come and ministers go; but I go on for ever.*

The scene is the English King's palace some time in the future. The Labour Cabinet are to meet him and offer an ultimatum: he must not refer again in public to the King's right of veto, which can seriously impede their government. The Cabinet includes a new minister, the Left Wing Boanerges, who arrives wearing Russian-style blouse and cap to meet King Magnus for the first time. He is flattered by the King's suave good manners and tactful recognition of his powers. The rest of the Cabinet, headed by Proteus, the Prime Minister, arrive and discuss the crisis. Magnus, confronted with the ultimatum, asks until five o'clock to consider his reply. He is, as Proteus realises, no fool and sympathetically inclined towards the problems of the Powermistress General, Lysistrata, whose efforts to run her department efficiently are continually undermined by Breakages Limited, a powerful firm whose financial well-being depends on contracts to repair machinery, and who buy up and suppress any inventions which might stem the flow of breakages and renewals.

In an Interlude we see Magnus relaxing with his mistress Orinthia. They have a strangely innocent relationship but she is insistent that he shall divorce his Queen—for whom he retains an obstinate affection—and marry her. A decorative, extravagant but intelligent woman, she is certain she will fit the role, whereas he feels she is better placed as at present, a fascinating diversion from cares of State and a happy but humdrum marriage. He insists on returning to his wife for tea, and in Orinthia's struggle to retain him they fall to the ground, fighting. In this undignified posture they are discovered by the King's secretary, Sempronius, who tactfully withdraws, knocks, re-enters and rescues the King, who goes off to tea.

Late that afternoon on the terrace, the King and Queen are visited by Vanhattan, the American Ambassador, who excitedly brings the news that his country has scrapped the Declaration of Independence and decided to rejoin the British Commonwealth. He is hurt that the King, realising that this virtually means a takeover bid for the British Isles, greets the news with modified rapture and asks time for consideration. The Cabinet arrive for the King's answer to their ultimatum. To their dismay he offers to abdicate in favour of his son, become a Commoner, form a new political party and stand as Parliamentary candidate for the Royal Borough of Windsor. Knowing that this new party would defeat him at the polls, Proteus tears up the ultimatum and admits defeat. When the Cabinet have gone, the Queen insists on Magnus's dressing for dinner and he allows himself to be gently bullied off the scene.

Too True to be Good (1931)

> *Nature never intended me for soldiering or thieving: I am by nature and destiny a preacher. I am the new Ecclesiastes. But I have no Bible, no creed: the war has shot both out of my hands.*

In a wealthy girl's sick room the Patient is sleeping and a Monster in an easy chair complains he is a microbe and she has given him German measles—not the other way about. Mrs. Mopply, the girl's mother, agonizes over her, and a young doctor, much derided by the Monster, defends his treatment. It is apparent that the girl is naturally healthy and has been cosseted into sickness; and her young, pretty Nurse suffers much from her petulance and the mother's fussing. The Nurse turns out to be a thief waiting for her friend, the Burglar, who appears in a mask and is promptly knocked down and winded by the Patient, who then faints. The Burglar decides against stealing the pearls and diamond ring and persuades the Patient to sell the jewels, join forces and escape. He is not a professional burglar but a young ex-army chaplain, secretly ordained because his father is an atheist. The Patient imagines she is dreaming and in love with him. They agree to pretend she has been kidnapped and demand a ransom. They flee with the jewels, and the Monster, transformed, proclaims both himself and the Patient cured.

In a mountainous Middle East country, Colonel Tall-boys is indulging his taste for painting in watercolours, while Private Meek runs army affairs and native negotiations, shattering the silence on his motor-bike. The expeditionary force has been sent to suppress brigandry and rescue a British lady held for ransom. Private Meek, to the Colonel's disbelief, reports that the last brigand retired 15 years ago. The Nurse, 'Sweetie', appears disguised as a countess, with the Patient as her native servant. The Burglar is also of the 'tourist' party. They have spent the £6,000 received for the necklace and now depend on the ransom. The Patient is bored and Meek translates her 'native dialect' to the Colonel as English backslang. The Colonel accuses the Patient of stealing some maroons. They are attacked by tribesmen and Meek briskly takes control, orders the firing of the 'missing' maroons from varied positions and frightens the attackers off. He offers to draw up a report for the Colonel who will get the D.S.O. It transpires that Meek has already given up three commissions and re-enlisted as a Private, and the Colonel is pleased to delegate authority and concentrate on his water colours.

Sweetie, attracted by Sergeant Fielding, finds him absorbed in the *Pilgrim's Progress* and the Bible, but not averse to flirtation. They are interrupted by the Elder, who springs from a cave proclaiming his lost dogmatic atheism and the doomed state of the world. He turns out to be the Burglar's father and is horrified to learn his son is a

clergyman. Mrs. Mopply, the Patient's mother, appears and
so exasperates the Colonel that he silences her by hitting her
over the head with an umbrella. Meek on his motor cycle
brings the news that the Colonel is made a k.c.b. Mrs.
Mopply, recovering from her blow, comes round, sees the
error of her past ways and strikes up a friendship with her
daughter, whom she doesn't recognise. Sweetie and the
Sergeant contemplate marriage. The Elder is reconciled to
his son's being a priest, in preference to a thief, and his son,
a compulsive preacher, launches into an oration on the
state of civilisation.

VILLAGE WOOING (1933)

On the lounge deck of the liner *Empress of Patagonia* a
talkative young woman on a cruise distracts a writer of
travelogues, known as the 'Marco Polo' man. She says she
is an assistant and telephone operator in a village shop,
that she won first prize in a newspaper competition and
decided to spend the lot in one go, living at the rate of
£5,000 a year.

   In a village shop and post office in Wiltshire, the 'Marco
Polo' man enters to buy groceries. He is served by the
young woman of the cruise, but at first does not recognise
her. He is persuaded to buy the store but resists her
attempts at marriage: he prefers to keep her on as a paid
employee. In the end, however, he finds her sexually
irresistible: the Life Force is at work.

ON THE ROCKS (1933)

> *You take it from me, you three gentlemen: all
> this country or any country has to stand between it
> and blue hell is the consciences of them that are
> capable of governing it.*

In the Cabinet Room of No. 10 Downing Street Sir

Arthur Chavender, the Prime Minister, and his secretary Hilda Hanways discuss the unemployed outside and the problem of the police in controlling them. Sir Broadfoot Basham, the Chief Commissioner of Police, advises against stopping street meetings but Sir Arthur, Liberal head of a Coalition Government, is worried by the reactions of his Tory colleagues. He is interrupted by his wife and two children, Flavia and David, who are quarrelling. Lady Chavender is sceptical about her husband's work and its value. She persuades him to see a lady doctor and go to her sanatorium in the Welsh mountains as he is on the verge of a nervous breakdown. An unemployed deputation visits him, including a hostile communist Oxford youth, Viscount Barking ('Toffy') and Alderwoman Aloysia Brollikins ('Brolly'), whom Chavender's children invite back to lunch. While Sir Arthur is attempting once again to compose a speech, a lady in grey appears, whom he at first takes for a ghost heralding his death. She proves to be the lady doctor and persuades him to go to her sanatorium, where he proposes to read Karl Marx, about whom the deputation have been talking.

On 10th November Basham and the right-wing Sir Dexter Rightside have come to No. 10 as a result of an inflammatory Marxist speech made by the Prime Minister at the Guildhall banquet. This demanded nationalisation of practically everything and delighted the unemployed. Sir Arthur is unrepentant. Basham subsides on learning that the speech also promised an increase of the police force and rises for himself and his men. Admiral Sir Bemrose Hotspot is similarly won over by promises of naval improvements, and a Scots M.P., a wealthy influential Cingalese, Sir Jafna Pandranath, and the Duke of Domesday are also impressed, for various reasons, by Sir Arthur's ideas. The Labour delegation returns: Barking is jubilant, the rest critical, especially on compulsory labour and the threat to the right to strike. Aloysia accuses Barking of wanting to marry Chavender's daughter, and although she also attacks the Duke of Domesday, the Duke is greatly impressed by her oratory. Barking blurts out that Aloysia herself intends to marry Chavender's son David.

Eventually Sir Arthur presents his plan: to prorogue parliament and put his reforms into practice. Sir Dexter threatens to oppose him with armed men in Union Jack shirts, and Basham threatens *him* with police support for the Prime Minister. Sir Dexter then resigns and declares the Coalition dissolved. His insult of Sir Jafna as a 'silly nigger' launches the Cingalese on a comparison of their civilisations, highly derogatory to the British, and he leaves to return to India. Most of the others feel bound to go and win back Sir Dexter, whom they consider indispensable. Sir Arthur is depressed and the Duke says he should have played golf on his holiday, instead of thinking. They are joined by the old socialist Hipney, who accompanied both delegations but prefers to settle business alone. He speaks of the failure of politics to gain the understanding or admiration of ordinary people, the contradictory statements of parliamentary leaders, and the public's misuse of its power to vote. In the end Sir Arthur, disillusioned, decides he is finished with parliament. Barking and Aloysia fix up their marriages with his children and he and his wife reflect on his retirement. There is a riot of unemployed outside, but without a leader they are easily dispersed, singing, not the Red Flag, but 'England arise!'

THE SIMPLETON OF THE UNEXPECTED ISLES (1934)

> *We shall plan commonwealths when our empires*
> *have brought us to the brink of destruction; but our*
> *plans will still lead us to the Unexpected Isles.*

In a Prologue, a young woman immigrant to the Un-

expected Isles, which have risen from the sea, bullies the
Emigration Officer, Hugo Hyering, demoralised by the
tropics, into accompanying her to the cliffs. They are met by
Pra, a handsome coloured priest, and Prola, a priestess, who
also impress an English male tourist and his wife, Sir
Charles and Lady Farwaters.

Twenty years later the six have, for eugenic purposes,
produced between them four beautiful coloured children,
two boys and two girls, intended to merge the finest of
eastern and western cultures. But the children, although
physically perfect and flawless in artistic taste, are without
moral conscience. A young clergyman left on the island by
pirates, who had kidnapped him, and known at home as
'Iddy', the idiot, is entranced by Maya, one of the children.
But on finding he is a 'nitrogen' baby (brought up by a
chemist father on products from nitrogen grass) Pra and
Prola decide he is the needed father of the next generation
in this experiment. Very reluctantly he is lured into union
with both girls, Maya and Vashti, who think of themselves
as one.

The unions however prove childless, and Maya and
Vashti are bored by Iddy. The Islands are threatened by
fleets of the world, the British demanding the handing
over of the bigamous clergyman, the Eastern peoples
wishing to protect him. A smallpox scare scatters them;
but a new visitor is an Angel announcing the Day of
Judgment. Telephonic news from England suggests satiric
chaos in the Cabinet, and the appearance of more angels.
The Angel says that lives which have no use, no meaning,
no purpose, will fade out, and news of sudden disappear-
ances in society is widespread. On the islands, Maya
vanishes in Iddy's arms, and her sister and brothers also.
Pra and Prola are left in their own curiously spiritual union,
realising their failure with their superchildren. In the
Unexpected Isles there is no security; and the future is to
those who prefer surprise and wonder to security.

THE SIX OF CALAIS (1934)

The historical story of the six burghers of Calais who offered themselves, in 1347, to King Edward III to be hanged, to save their town and its inhabitants from the King's vengeance following a long siege, and of the pleading of the Queen, Philippa of Hainault, which saved their lives, is dramatised by Shaw, but with a typical Shavian twist. One of the Burghers, Peter (or Piers) de Rosty, defies the King with such spirit and contempt, mocking him as henpecked, that the Queen finds herself in this case demanding punishment. But the King, his anger appeased, is tickled by the man's defiance, especially when he finds that, like his own grandmother, he hails from 'lousy Champagne'. The King this time has his way, and the play ends with the whole camp laughing while Peter brays like a donkey, having reduced the King's name to 'Neddy'.

THE MILLIONAIRESS (1935)

I think Allah loves those who make money.

Epifania Fitzfassenden, a millionairess, calls on a solicitor, threatening suicide and wishing to make a will leaving all to her husband, Alastair, whom she thinks the money will ruin. He had fulfilled, by trickery, her father's suggestion that she should only marry a man who could turn £150 into £50,000 in six months, but now his purely physical attractions have waned for her and he is involved with another woman. Sagamore, the solicitor, laughs her out of suicide, and Alastair and his new interest, Patricia Smith, arrive, asking for a separation from Epifania.

In a riverside inn Epifania quarrels with her own admirer, Adrian Blenderbland, on the subject of her father-fixation, and punches him downstairs. Collapsing, she is found by an Egyptian doctor who resists her urgent demands for succour and attention, as his serious work is for the poor.

She offers to marry him but he says he is married to science, and his mother made him promise only to marry a woman who could go into the world with nothing but the 200 piastres (35 shillings) he gave her and earn her living unaided for six months. Epifania accepts the test and blackmails herself into a job in a basement sweatshop. Within an hour she has used her business knowledge to by-pass the middleman and deal directly with the wholesalers, and is in practical control.

Beginning as scullery maid, she also takes over and transforms and modernises the riverside inn. Alastair and Patricia, happily staying there as man and wife, learn of this and meet Adrian (still on crutches, and claiming damages) and Sagamore. Epifania is infuriated that Alastair and Patricia are using her name, and by Adrian's lawsuit, but is physically quelled by Alastair. Epifania orders Sagamore to get her a divorce so that she can marry the Egyptian doctor, and points out that she has fulfilled the doctor's condition. But the doctor can see only the continued cheap labour at the workshop, and the unhappy old hotel owners she has driven out, and says 'the wrath of Allah shall overtake those who leave the world no better than they found it'. He has spent her £150 on saving from penury the widow of his scientific mentor, and thus not fulfilled her own condition; but Epifania contends that the scientist's invention has made more than £50,000 for others, and thus the doctor's gift, which helped the widow launch it, was responsible for this. The doctor in the end can resist her money, but not her strong and unique pulse, a medical curiosity. Sagamore is told to arrange the divorce and marriage.

CYMBELINE REFINISHED (1937)

This is a shortened, more comedic version of Shakespeare's last Act, retaining some of the original verse but

resolving the complex plot with different character reactions. Avigarius and Guiderius, revealed to be the stolen
sons of Cymbeline, repudiate their princehood and right to
inherit the throne, preferring their cave and the animals to
human sycophants. Imogen does not so easily forgive
Posthumus his attempt to murder her and his easy belief
in her guilt as a wife, and is only reconciled after Iachimo
has told her the story of the chest and pleaded for Posthumus.

> He has his faults; but he must suffer yours.
> You are, I swear, a very worthy lady,
> But still, not quite an angel.

Of the wicked Queen's machinations and death we hear
nothing.

Geneva (1938)

> *The trial of the dictators by the Permanent Court*
> *of International Justice has been fixed for this day*
> *fortnight.*

In the office of the Committee for Intellectual Co-operation
in Geneva the English typist in charge is visited in turn by
two men and a widow, complaining of dictators and family
blood feuds in their respective countries. Taking her cue
from the first, a Jew, she suggests the cases should be tried
at the International Court at the Hague. A Bishop concerned about his footman, a Communist, is shocked to
meet a Russian Commissar lodging a complaint about a
British organisation within Russia attempting to over-
throw the system. At the final shock of learning there are
no poor in Russia the Bishop drops dead.

In the office of the Secretary of the League of Nations
the Secretary receives the English typist, Begonia Brown.
Her only interest in his news of world unrest and war by

sanctions is that the British flag has been dishonoured; and she is flattered by his information that she caused this world holocaust by her letters to the Court of International Justice at the Hague. She is followed by Sir Orpheus Midlander, British Foreign Secretary, and the Senior Judge of the Hague Court, who says the four cases are to be tried; the letters have provided an opportunity he has long awaited to devise a judicial procedure by which political lawbreakers may be brought to justice. The Secretary and Midlander are then interrupted by Begonia with the news that she has been adopted as Conservative candidate for a Camberwell by-election, as Midlander's nephew, to whom she is engaged, does not wish to stand. They recognise that her typical British attitudes will win her the seat.

At a Geneva restaurant the latest doings of Begonia (now a Dame of the British Empire) are discussed. Midlander brings in the Catholic blood feud widow who shows intolerance by wishing to shoot the Jew. They are joined by Begonia, the Commissar and the Judge. Their discussions are mainly based on national self-interest and the Secretary of the League says they are all enemies of the human race. They pair off for dinner and the Judge tells the Secretary, who doubts it, that the dictators will come for their trial at the Hague: 'Where the spotlight is, there will the despots be gathered.'

At the Hague Court all commiserate with the Judge on the empty hall but he genially disconcerts them by explaining that they are all on television, which he has arranged to avoid a crowd in Court. The dictator Bombardone arrives, followed by Battler. Both are incredulous at Midlander's honeyed diplomacy, which nevertheless dares to menace them should they move to attack England. The Judge indicts the bombing of civilians and laying of mines. Midlander says they are a terrible necessity, and compares them to accidents on roads and in the air: we cannot give up flying and travelling because of them. But the Judge insists there is a difference: those accidents are not a planned part of flying and travelling, as bombing is of war. And populations no longer replace those killed in war; the pregnant woman, too, is the target of the bombs. A Deaconess intrudes in the name of Jesus, preaching universal love, but is rejected by the dictators who consider they have replaced God. General Flanco arrives and faces a charge of bringing devastation and war to his own country, but he says it was to get rid of the democratic cads and ensure government by gentlemen. Battler resists the accusations of the Jew, claiming divine leadership. The Commissar points out that the dictators' own peoples do not own the land they starve in. They are owned by a handful of landlords and capitalists who exploit them. Midlander and the dictators threaten each other with bombing or retaliation, and the Judge condemns them all for irrational scoundrelism when it comes to foreign policy.

It is announced that Battler's troops have invaded Ruritania and he is outraged that Bombardone and Flanco refuse to support him to make him 'emperor of the universe'. News is brought that the earth has jumped into its next quantum, out of the range of the sun, and all will be frozen to death. Everyone leaves to organise his countrymen's deaths. Left alone, the Secretary remarks to the Judge that one has only to mention Science and men will believe anything. 'It broke up this farce of a trial, at all events.' But the Judge replies it was not a farce. 'They came, these fellows. They blustered: they defied us. But they came.'

'In Good King Charles's Golden Days' (1939)

How often have I told you that I am no real King: that the utmost I can do is to keep my crown on my head and my head on my shoulders.

At Sir Isaac Newton's house in Cambridge, 1680, his housekeeper Mrs. Basham is annoyed by the visit of a tall, dark, mysterious 'Mr. Rowley', with a pack of dogs, and George Fox, founder of the Society of Friends, or Quakers. Newton is delighted: he recognises 'Mr. Rowley' as the name by which King Charles II is known when incognito. They are joined by Nell Gwynn, whose warm good nature and tact disarm even Fox, and Barbara, Duchess of Cleveland, a more tempestuous and jealous mistress of Charles.

Charles's third mistress, the French Louise de Kéroualle, arrives and demands a love potion from Newton, who she takes to be an alchemist. He staves her off with a harmless prescription. Charles's brother James, Duke of York, then calls, and he and Newton, falling out over Galileo and Popery, are fighting on the floor when Charles returns. Newton leaves the royal brothers, and Charles warns James of the dangers of his bigoted and uncompromising attitude when he succeeds to the throne. He admits he himself is no King in James's sense: 'To be what you call a king I lack military ambition; and I lack cruelty.' But he has learnt Kingcraft in a more subtle way. He recommends young Jack Churchill to James as a potential general, and is distressed by James's belief that his bastard son, Monmouth, plots against them both.

They are interrupted by Mrs. Basham, exasperated that everyone is staying to lunch, and are joined by a further visitor, Godfrey Kneller, the painter. The others return and are diverted by Nell's acting from Dryden, but Fox is horrified at the greater pay and homage given to mere players than to religious leaders. Barbara tears up an unflattering drawing made of her by Kneller, and Kneller is angry with Newton, saying his scientific analysis of the first law of motion, that it is based on a straight line, is totally wrong: as an artist he instinctively knows 'motion in a curve is the law of nature'. Newton is appalled to find his life's work invalidated if this is true. He is still, however, able to confuse Kneller with the time faults of the universe, the sidereal clock and the perihelion of Mercury. They talk themselves out of the room, to lunch.

Charles has taken refuge in the boudoir of his Queen, Catherine of Braganza. He increasingly values his wife above other women, is concerned for her safety as a Catholic and warns her she must return to Portugal after his death, for the English Protestants will soon get rid of James and the Protestant William of Orange will become King. She is upset at his talk of death and dismisses his unfaithfulness, knowing she means more to him than any of his mistresses. She has, says Charles, brains and character. She knows she could govern Portugal and should make Charles divorce her so he can get an heir, but is too fond of him to leave him. She helps valet him and sends him out to a Council meeting.

BUOYANT BILLIONS (1948)

Love marriages are the most unreasonable, and probably the most often regretted.

Junius Smith is the seventh son of a seventh son and the mystic tradition associated with this tells him that 'the world has a future that will make its people look back on us as a mob of starving savages'. He sees himself as a 'world betterer' in revolt against the system, in particular the system of rich and poor. His father argues for constitutional means of change, but the son says the object of revolution is to change the constitution: 95 per cent of the voting public understand nothing of politics, but are guided by leaders; and they vote for the worst leaders—for Titus Oates and Lord George Gordon, for Hitlers and Mussolinis who exterminate Jews or rally them to nationalist dreams of glory and empire. 'Within the last 30 years we have had more horrible persecutions and massacres, more diabolical tortures and crucifixions, more slaughter and destruction than Attila and Genghis Khan and all the other scourges of God ever ventured on.' But atomic power will control mankind, which 'has not the nerve to go through to the end with murder and suicide'. Already Hiroshima and Nagasaki are rebuilt, and atomic power can be used to make life more worth living. Junius says he would like to go round the world to investigate its use in ridding us of the mosquito, the tsetse fly and the locust, with particular attention to the region of the Panama Canal. His father gives him the fare and they part with affection.

In a tropical Panama landscape Junius asks a young woman for shelter and food in her wooden house. She orders him away and slams the door, but milk and fruit are delivered by a native: Junius pays him to bring him some. He learns that the girl is believed holy, a magician who speaks with spirits, and manages to converse with her again. She tells him she learned the soprano saxophone and can charm snakes and alligators to drive him off. She has deliberately escaped from civilisation after reading Marx. She and Smith find they are both born of men who started as proletarian tradesmen, and made money. She resists his advances and slams the door again. He discusses religion with the philosopher-native. The girl frightens both away by playing the saxophone and attracting an alligator.

At a house in Belgrave Square, Sir Ferdinand Flopper, the solicitor of the billionaire Buoyant, is shown by a Chinese priest into a room decorated as a Chinese temple. The priest explains it is for Buoyant's private rest and meditation and he wishes Flopper to meet his family here. The family (three sons, a daughter and daughters-in-law) learn that their father's untaxed millions, made on the stock market, will be taxed when he dies and they will have to reduce their standard of living, and work by taking directorships. Buoyant's elder daughter is provided for, and the family tell Flopper she was the daughter of the first marriage when Buoyant was poor, is no lady, and can do all the things, like housework, they are incapable of. She is now in Panama, living alone in a shack. She (Clementina), however, returns and confesses she has run away from a man because she was falling in love with him. Soon afterwards the man, Junius Smith, is announced and confesses he is mad about her and must marry her. The girl says she dare not marry him—she loves him and would become his slave. But after a great deal of discussion, and with the blessing of old Bill Buoyant, the Life Force wins and the marriage is arranged.

SHAKES VERSUS SHAV (1949)

'A puppet play.' This return to Shakespearean pastiche and quotation was Shaw's last playlet (at the age of 93). Shakes and Shav fight, as do Rob Roy (suggested by Shav as Macbeth's equal) and Macbeth. Shav succeeds in making Shakes laugh and matches his Shotover with Shakespeare's Lear. Shav in the end says:

> We both are mortal. For a moment suffer
> My glimmering light to shine.

And with the words 'Out, out, brief candle', Shakespeare blows out the light that appears between them, leaving only darkness.

FARFETCHED FABLES (1950)

The pursuit of knowledge and power will never end.

FIRST FABLE. A young man and woman, at first attracted, meet on a park bench and discuss war and the atomic bomb. The woman will not marry because she refuses to bring children into a world of such horrors. If atomic bombs are not used in the next war, because of their danger to both sides, 'somebody', she says, 'will discover a poison gas lighter than air'. It may kill the inhabitants of a city; but it will leave the city standing and in working order. The young man, a chemist in a chlorine gas factory, is struck with the possibilities of the idea, and she leaves him dreaming of the financial reward to the inventor.

SECOND FABLE. At the War Office the Commander-in-Chief, Ulsterbridge, and Lord Oldhand from the Foreign Office, discuss the killing of all the inhabitants of the Isle of Wight by volatile poison gas. Oldhand says it is all Ulsterbridge's fault, for refusing to pay the inventor of the gas the £100,000 he asked; so he sold the invention to the African Hitler, Ketchewayo the Second, who has used it to show Cape Town and the rest of the world they are at his mercy. The inventor went to live in the Isle of Wight for safety and has perished from his own gas. As they argue, an artillery salvo is heard, gas seeps through the window, and they die singing.

THIRD FABLE. Outside the Anthropometric Laboratory on the Isle of Wight, a middle-aged gentleman, the matron and a junior interview and recruit a tourist and a tramp who have gained illegal entry to the island. Their work is to classify men and women according to their abilities. The tourist is sure he can do the job easily and paint like a genius in his spare time. The tramp resists the idea of work, says he will be useless, but yields for food in the canteen. The gentleman rejoices in two big catches: 'A nincompoop who thinks he's a genius; and a genius who thinks he's a nincompoop'. The matron is disturbed, because you never know what a genius will be up to next.

FOURTH FABLE. The Isle of Wight again. The building is now inscribed 'Diet Commissioners'. A Commissioner in cap and gown is dictating into a dictaphone a thesis for the tenth edition of his primer on rudimentary biology. It describes the progress in feeding habits of mankind from meat-eating to pure vegetarianism, by which men became grass-eaters with savage natures like supergorillas and bulls, but no organised war. They were healthier and lived longer, but the processes of illness and death continued, until a Russian woman athlete discovered the possibilities of living on air and water. Men and women were now no longer the slaves of nature. 'The supergorilla became the soldier and servant of Creative Evolution'.

FIFTH FABLE. Elsewhere on the Isle of Wight is a building labelled 'Genetic Institute'. Two men, a woman and a hermaphrodite, all in the prime of life, are reading books of the nineteenth century and finding the life of that time, and in particular its total failure to mention sex, incomprehensible. The woman explains that their reproductive processes were then quite different and rather horrifying, unlike their own use of seminal fluids made by their chemists in the laboratory. But they themselves are descended from those primitive savages and have not yet agreed on the sort of mankind they ought to manufacture. The hermaphrodite protests that it wants to get rid of the body and become pure mind, but the woman says that will still only be like picking up another grain of sand. The man says, 'In the infinity of time, when the oceans dry up and make no more sand, we shall pick them all up.'

SIXTH AND LAST FABLE. An Isle of Wight building is labelled 'Sixth Form School. Scheduled Historic Monument'. Youths and maidens question with their teacher their differences of mentality and ability, and where thoughts come from. They are an atavistic civilisation, a throwback to the twentieth century. There is a legend which some believe, and some doubt, of a previous Disembodied Race that dispensed with the body and became a vortex of thought. Some think that the thoughts that come into their heads—a process which cannot be rationally explained—come from them. The Disembodied Race are still using them in their pursuit of knowledge and power. One points out that this pursuit has led them to destructions and wars. The teacher asks, 'What is an immortal soul but a disembodied thought?' They are visited by a feathered youth named Raphael, one of the disembodied now incarnate. He says he is curious to experience the body, and curiosity never dies. He has none of their bodily passions but 'intellectual passion, mathematical passion, passion for discovery and exploration: the mightiest of all the passions'. When he vanishes, the teacher advises them to read an old poem called The Book of Job.

WHO'S WHO

'A'. Author of the 'Marco Polo' series of travel guide books, trying to work on a pleasure cruise. 'A literary-looking pale gentleman under forty.'—*Village Wooing*.

ACHILLAS. Historical character. General of troops of boy king Ptolemy. 'Apparently not a clever man, but distinguished and dignified.'—*Caesar and Cleopatra*.

ACIS. Youth of nearly three years, 31,920 A.D. *Back to Methuselah* ('As Far as Thought Can Reach').

ADAM. Biblical character, the first man, learning of death and the burden of eternal life in the Garden of Eden.— *Back to Methuselah* ('In the Beginning').

AIRE, JEAN D'. Historical character. One of six burghers. —*The Six of Calais*.

ALICE, PRINCESS. The young Princess Royal of England, Magnus's daughter.—*The Apple Cart*.

AMANDA. Postmistress General. 'A merry lady in uniform' who gains political advantage from a talent for mimicry.—*The Apple Cart*.

AMARYLLIS. 'The Newly-Born', 31,920 A.D. A girl-baby of about 17 years (in our terms), born on stage from an egg.—*Back to Methuselah* ('As Far as Thought Can Reach').

ANDERSON, ANTHONY. Husband of Judith. 'A shrewd, genial, ready Presbyterian divine of about 50.'—*The Devil's Disciple*.

ANDERSON, JUDITH. Young wife of Anthony, romantically in love with Dick Dudgeon. 'She is pretty and proper and ladylike, and has been admired and petted into an opinion of herself sufficiently favourable to give her a self-assurance which serves her instead of strength.'— *The Devil's Disciple.*

ANDROCLES. Greek tailor and Christian devoted to animals, who takes a thorn out of the paw of a wounded lion, with surprising results. 'A small, thin, ridiculous little man who might be any age from 30 to 55.'—*Androcles and the Lion.*

ANGEL, THE. Angel of the Last Judgment, visitant to the Isles.—*The Simpleton of the Unexpected Isles.*

ANNAJANSKA, GRAND DUCHESS. Daughter of the Panjandrum of Beotia, she has joined the Revolution and become the Bolshevik Empress. 'If the people cannot govern themselves, they must be governed by somebody. If they will not do their duty without being half forced and half humbugged, somebody must force them and humbug them.'—*Annajanska, The Bolshevik Empress.*

APJOHN, HENRY ('HE'). Poet naïvely in love with a married woman. 'A very beautiful youth, moving as in a dream, walking on air.'—*How He Lied To Her Husband.*

APOLLODORUS. Sicilian carpet trader and art lover. 'A dashing young man of about 24, handsome and debonair, dressed with deliberate aestheticism.'—*Caesar and Cleopatra.*

ARCHBISHOP OF RHEIMS. Historical character who officiated at the coronation of the Dauphin. 'A full-fed political prelate with nothing of the ecclesiastic about him except his imposing bearing.'—*Saint Joan.*

ARCHBISHOP OF YORK. Long-liver of 283 years, formerly the Rev. Bill Haslam (*q.v.*). 'He does not look a day over 50, and is very well preserved even at that; but his boyishness of manner is quite gone; he now has complete authority and self-possession.'—*Back to Methuselah* ('The Thing Happens').

ARJILLAX. Sculptor, 31,920 A.D. Nearing adolescence and beginning to create statues of the Ancients in preference to ones of beautiful young people.—*Back to Methuselah* ('As Far As Thought Can Reach').

AUFSTEIG, GENERAL. A General, 3000 A.D., resembling and dressed as Napoleon. Military genius, Emperor of Turania, who has come to consult the Oracle.—*Back to Methuselah* ('Tragedy of an Elderly Gentleman').

'AUNT JUDY'. 'A woman of 50 . . . lively and busy without energy or grip, placid without tranquillity, kindly without concern for others.'—*John Bull's Other Island.*

BABSY. 'A bumptious young slattern.'—*The Shewing-up of Blanco Posnet.*

BADGER-BLUEBIN, British Envoy and Prime Minister who has come to consult the Oracle, 3000 A.D. 'A typical politician, looks like an imperfectly reformed criminal disguised by a good tailor.'—*Back to Methuselah* ('Tragedy of an Elderly Gentleman').

BAINES, MRS. Salvation Army Commissioner. 'An earnest-looking woman of about 40.'—*Major Barbara.*

BAKER, JULIUS. (*See* GUNNER)—*Misalliance.*

BALBUS. Home Secretary. 'Rude and thoughtless.'—*The Apple Cart.*

BALSQUITH. Prime Minister.—*Press Cuttings.*

BANGER, MRS. Secretary of Anti-Suffragette League. 'A masculine woman of 40.'—*Press Cuttings.*

BANNAL, FLAWNER. Critic of 20. 'Obviously an unemployable of the business class picking up a living by an obtuse courage, which gives him cheerfulness, conviviality, and bounce, and is helped out positively by a slight turn for writing and negatively by a comfortable ignorance and lack of intuition.'—*Fanny's First Play.*

BARKING, VISCOUNT ('TOFFY'). A Communist in love with Flavia Chavender. 'A powerfully built, loud voiced young man fresh from Oxford University, defying convention in corduroys, pullover, and unshaven black beard.' —*On the Rocks.*

BARNABAS. Accountant-General of the British Islands, 2170 A.D. Remote descendant of the Brothers Barnabas. 'He is rather like Conrad Barnabas, but younger, and much more commonplace.'—*Back to Methuselah* ('The Thing Happens').

BARNABAS, CONRAD. Professor of Biology at Jarrowfields University. Author of a book on creative evolution, suggesting that by subconscious will human beings should extend their life span to three hundred years.—*Back to Methuselah* ('The Gospel of the Brothers Barnabas').

BARNABAS, FRANKLYN. Ex-cleric brother of Conrad, and fellow advocate of the longevity theory. 'An impressive-looking gentleman of 50.'—*Back to Methuselah* ('The Gospel of the Brothers Barnabas').

BARNABAS, 'SAVVY' (short for 'Savage'). Daughter of Franklyn, later married to the Rev. William Haslam. 'A vigorous sunburnt young lady with hazel hair cut to the level of her neck, like an Italian youth in a Gozzoli picture.'—*Back to Methuselah* ('The Gospel of the Brothers Barnabas').

BASHAM, SIR BROADFOOT. Chief Commissioner of Police. 'A capable looking man from the military point of view. He is a gentleman.'—*On the Rocks.*

BASHAM, MRS. Sir Isaac Newton's housekeeper.—*In Good King Charles's Golden Days.*

BASHVILLE. Lydia Carew's footman, in love with her.—*The Admirable Bashville.*

BASTABLE, AUGUSTUS. Lover of Lady Magnesia, petrified by poison and lime plaster antidote.—*Passion, Poison and Petrifaction.*

BATTLER, ERNEST. Ruthless, neurotic Aryan dictator, satirically based on Hitler. 'An unsmiling middle-aged gentleman with slim figure, erect carriage, and resolutely dissatisfied expression.'—*Geneva.*

BAUDRICOURT, CAPTAIN ROBERT DE. Historical character who provided Joan of Arc with soldiers to go to the Dauphin. 'A military squire, handsome and physically energetic, but with no will of his own.'—*Saint Joan.*

BEAMISH. Old clerk at Little Pifflington Town Hall.—*Augustus Does His Bit.*

BEEFEATER. Warden on guard at Whitehall Palace, not impressed by a bribe to enable him to see the 'newfangled' plays of William Shakespeare.—*The Dark Lady of the Sonnets.*

BEL AFFRIS. Egyptian soldier. 'A fairhaired dandy.'— *Caesar and Cleopatra.*

BELZANOR. Veteran captain of Cleopatra's guard. 'An effective sergeant, an incompetent general, a deplorable dictator.'—*Caesar and Cleopatra.*

BETROTHED, THE ('BENJY'). Nephew of Sir Orpheus Midlander, engaged to Begonia Brown. 'A cheerful young gentleman' of doubtful intellect.—*Geneva.*

BILTON. A foreman at the Undershaft armaments factory.—*Major Barbara.*

BISHOP, THE. Shocked literally to death by meeting with Bolshevik Commissar. 'Old, soft, gentle and rather infirm.'—*Geneva.*

BLACK PRINCE, THE (EDWARD, PRINCE OF WALES) (1330–1376). Aged 17.—*The Six of Calais.*

BLEE, ALDERMAN. 'A thin, undersized lower middle class young man . . . evidently with a good conceit of himself.'—*On the Rocks.*

BLENDERBLAND, ADRIAN. 'An imposing man in the prime of life, bearded in the Victorian literary fashion.'— *The Millionairess.*

BLENKINSOP, DR. General practitioner in poor district of London, suffering from tuberculosis. 'He has the lines made by a conscience between his eyes, and the lines made by continual money worries all over his face.'—*The Doctor's Dilemma.*

BLUNTSCHLI. Swiss volunteer in the Serbian army, Raina's 'chocolate cream soldier.' 'A man of about 35 . . . with all his wits about him in spite of his desperate predicament: even with a sense of the humour of it.'—*Arms and the Man*.

BOANERGES. President of the Board of Trade, newly elected to the Cabinet: a Left Winger, fancying himself as a Strong Man, dressed in Russian blouse and peaked cap. 'He is 50, heavily built and aggressively self-assertive.'— *The Apple Cart*.

BOHUN, Q.C. Brilliant lawyer son of Bohun, the head waiter, Marine Hotel. 'A tall, stout man between 40 and 50 . . . Physically and spiritually a coarsened man, in cunning and logic a ruthlessly sharpened one.'—*You Never Can Tell*.

BOHUN, WALTER (called 'William' by the Clandon twins). Head waiter of the Marine Hotel. Father of Bohun, Q.C. 'A silky old man, white-haired and delicate-looking, but so cheerful and contented that in his encouraging presence ambition stands rebuked as vulgarity . . . He has a certain expression peculiar to men who are pre-eminent in their callings.'—*You Never Can Tell*.

BOMBARDONE, BARDO. Latin dictator, satirically based on Mussolini. 'Dominant, brusque, every inch a man of destiny.'—*Geneva*.

BOMPAS, AURORA ('SHE'). A married woman loved by a young poet and fearing discovery. 'A very ordinary South Kensington female of about 37' with 'spoilt, petted ways'. —*How He Lied To Her Husband*.

BOMPAS, 'TEDDY' ('HER HUSBAND'). 'A robust, thick-necked, well groomed city man.'—*How He Lied To Her Husband*.

BONINGTON, SIR RALPH BLOOMFIELD ('B.B.'). Royal physician who has accidentally cured a prince. '. . . his speech is a perpetual anthem; and he never tires of the sound of it . . . Even broken bones, it is said, have been known to unite at the sound of his voice.'—*The Doctor's Dilemma*.

BOSHINGTON, SIR CARDONIUS. Lord Chancellor.—*The Fascinating Foundling*.

BRABAZON, HORACE. A foundling. 'A smart and beautiful young man of 19, dressed in the extremity of fashion.'—*The Fascinating Foundling*.

BRASSBOUND, CAPTAIN. Wronged nephew of Hallam, seeking revenge. 'Age about 36. Handsome features, but joyless . . . a face set to one tragic purpose. A man of few words, fewer gestures, and much significance.'—*Captain Brassbound's Conversion*.

BRIDGENORTH, ALFRED, BISHOP OF CHELSEA. 'Younger by temperament than his brothers. He has clever, humorous eyes . . . ready bright speech, and the ways of a successful man who is always interested in himself and generally rather well pleased with himself.'—*Getting Married*.

BRIDGENORTH, EDITH. Daughter of the Bishop of Chelsea. 'The typical spoilt child of a clerical household . . . her impetuous temper and energetic will . . . carry everything before them.'—*Getting Married*.

BRIDGENORTH, GENERAL (BOXER). The Bishop of Chelsea's brother. 'He is ignorant, stupid and prejudiced, having been carefully trained to be so . . . but one blames society, not himself, for this.'—*Getting Married.*

BRIDGENORTH, LEO. Divorced wife of Reginald. 'Very pretty, very youthful, very restless . . . a born fusser about herself and everybody else for whom she feels responsible.'—*Getting Married.*

BRIDGENORTH, MRS. The Bishop of Chelsea's wife.— *Getting Married.*

BRIDGENORTH, REGINALD. Divorced husband of Leo, eldest brother of the Bishop of Chelsea. 'He is a muddled, rebellious, hasty, untidy, forgetful, always late sort of man, who very evidently needs the care of a capable woman.'— *Getting Married.*

BRITANNUS. A Briton acting as secretary to Caesar. 'About 40, tall, solemn.'—*Caesar and Cleopatra.*

BRITISH ENVOY (AMBROSE). Visitor to Galway with his wife and daughter.—*Back to Methuselah* ("Tragedy of an Elderly Gentleman').

BROADBENT, TOM. Civil engineer. 'A robust, full-blooded, energetic man in the prime of life, sometimes eager and credulous . . . always buoyant and irresistible, mostly likeable, and enormously absurd in his most earnest moments.'—*John Bull's Other Island.*

BROLLIKINS, ALOYSIA ('BROLLY'). Socialist Alderwoman in love with David Chavender. 'An unladylike but brilliant and very confident young woman in smart,

factory-made clothes after the latest Parisian models.'—
On the Rocks.

BROWN, BEGONIA. Typist at Committee for Intellectual
Co-Operation, Geneva; later M.P. for Camberwell and
Dame of the British Empire. 'A self-satisfied young person,
fairly attractive and well aware of it.'—*Geneva.*

BUOYANT, CLEMENTINA ALEXANDRA ('SHE'). Eldest
daughter of Bill Buoyant, living alone in Panama and in
love with Junius Smith.—*Buoyant Billions.*

BUOYANT, EUDOXIA EMILY ('DARKIE'). Younger daughter of Bill Buoyant: aged 20.—*Buoyant Billions.*

BUOYANT, FREDERICK ('FIFFY'). Youngest son of Bill
Buoyant. 'An irreverent youth of 17.'—*Buoyant Billions.*

BUOYANT, 'OLD BILL'. Self-made billionaire. 'A greybeard, like any other greybeard; but a gorgeous golden
dressing gown and yellow slippers give him a hieratic
air.'—*Buoyant Billions.*

BURGE, JOYCE. Liberal Party leader out of office. 'He
screws up his cheeks into a smile at each introduction, and
makes his eyes shine in a very winning manner.'—*Back to
Methuselah* ('The Gospel of the Brothers Barnabas').

BURGE-LUBIN. President of the British Islands, 2170 A.D.
Remote descendant of Joyce Burge and Lubin. 'He is like
Joyce Burge, yet also like Lubin, as if Nature had made a
composite photograph of the two.'—*Back to Methuselah*
('The Thing Happens').

BURGESS, MR. Candida's father, employer of cheap
labour. 'A vulgar ignorant guzzling man.'—*Candida.*

BURGLAR, THE. Young, good looking, ex-army chaplain turned thief with a compulsive gift for preaching (later disguised as the Hon. Aubrey Bagot).—*Too True To Be Good*.

BURGOYNE, GENERAL JOHN. Historical character (1723–1792). Commander of British forces defeated at Saratoga, American War of Independence, 1777, owing to failure of War Office to send dispatches for reinforcements. Known as 'Gentlemanly Johnny'. 'General Burgoyne is 55, and very well preserved. He is a man of fashion, gallant enough to have made a distinguished marriage by an elopement, witty enough to write successful comedies . . . His eyes, large, brilliant, apprehensive and intelligent, are his most remarkable feature . . . A man who plays his part in life, and makes all its points, in the manner of a born high comedian.'—*Devil's Disciple*.

BYRON, CASHEL. Prizefighter son of Adelaide Gisborne; in love with Lydia Carew.—*The Admirable Bashville*.

CADI, THE. Moroccan overlord of Sidi el Assif. 'A vigorous, fatfeatured, choleric, whitehaired and bearded elder.'—*Captain Brassbound's Conversion*.

CAESAR, JULIUS. Historical character (100 or 102 B.C.–44 B.C.).'Nobody need deny Caesar a share, at least, of the qualities I have attributed to him', wrote Shaw.—*Caesar and Cleopatra*.

CAIN. Biblical character, the first murderer. 'In pose, voice, and dress he is insistently warlike . . . To his parents he has the self-assertive, not-quite-at-ease manner of a revolted son who knows that he is not forgiven nor approved of.'—*Back to Methuselah* ('In the Beginning').

CANDIDA. Wife of the Rev. James Morell 'A woman of 33 ... now quite at her best, with the double charm of youth and motherhood. Her ways are those of a woman who has found that she can always manage people by engaging their affection.'—*Candida.*

CAPTAIN, THE. Friend to Lavinia, the Christian. 'A patrician, handsome, about 35, very cold and distinguished, very superior and authoritative.'—*Androcles and the Lion.*

CAREW, LYDIA. Highborn lady in love with Cashel Byron.—*The Admirable Bashville.*

CATHERINE II, Empress of Russia (1729–1796). 'She not only disputes with Frederick the Great the reputation of being the cleverest monarch in Europe, but may even put in a very plausible claim to be the cleverest and most attractive individual alive.'—*Great Catherine.*

CATHERINE OF BRAGANZA (1638–1705). Portuguese princess, wife of Charles II, aged 42.—*In Good King Charles's Golden Days.*

CAUCHON, PETER, BISHOP OF BEAUVAIS. Historical character, 'aged about 60', who headed the tribunal at the trial of Joan of Arc.—*Saint Joan.*

CENTURION. In charge of the Christian prisoners' escort. —*Androcles and the Lion.*

CETEWAYO. Historical character. Zulu chieftain, died 1884. Present at Cashel Byron's fight at Islington.— *The Admirable Bashville.*

CHARLES II (1630–1685). King of England, known when incognito as Mr. Rowley.—*In Good King Charles's Golden Days*.

CHARMIAN. Historical character. Favourite servant to Cleopatra. 'A hatchet faced, terra cotta coloured little goblin, swift in her movements.'—*Caesar and Cleopatra*.

CHARTERIS, LEONARD. The 'philanderer' of the title, about 35 years old. 'The arrangement of his tawny hair, and of his moustaches and short beard, is apparently left to Nature; but he has taken care that Nature shall do him the fullest justice.'—*The Philanderer*.

CHAVENDER, SIR ARTHUR. Prime Minister in a Coalition Government. 'He has an orator's voice of pleasant tone; and his manners are very genial.'—*On the Rocks*.

CHAVENDER, DAVID. The Prime Minister's son. '18, slight, refined.'—*On the Rocks*.

CHAVENDER, FLAVIA. The Prime Minister's daughter, aged 19.—*On the Rocks*.

CHAVENDER, LADY. The Prime Minister's wife. 'She is a nice woman, and good looking; but she is bored, and her habitual manner is one of apology for being not only unable to take an interest in people, but even to pretend that she does.'—*On the Rocks*.

CHLOE. Maiden of four years old, 31,920 A.D. About to mature and throw away childish pleasures like love and the arts.—*Back to Methuselah* ('As Far As Thought Can Reach').

CLAIRE. Socially-conscious young English lady in St. Petersburg, fiancée of Captain Edstaston.—*Great Catherine.*

CLANDON, DOLLY. Voluble 18-year-old twin of Philip. 'A very pretty woman in miniature.'—*You Never Can Tell.*

CLANDON, GLORIA. Sister of the twins. 'A mettlesome dominative character paralysed by the inexperience of her youth . . . Unlike her mother, she is all passion; and the conflict of her passion with her obstinate pride and intense fastidiousness results in a freezing coldness of manner.'— *You Never Can Tell.*

CLANDON, MRS. Authoress on women's rights and mother of the twins and Gloria. 'A woman of cultivated interests rather than passionately developed personal affections.' —*You Never Can Tell.*

CLANDON, PHILIP. 18-year-old twin of Dolly. 'A handsome man in miniature', as voluble as his sister, 'with perfect manners and a finished personal style which might be envied by a man twice his age. Suavity and self-possession are points of honour with him.'—*You Never Can Tell.*

CLEOPATRA. Historical character (69 B.C.–30 B.C.). Daughter of the Egyptian king of Greek dynasty, Ptolemy, who died 51 B.C. Cleopatra under his will should have succeeded him jointly with her brother Ptolemy but was expelled by Ptolemy's guardians. Caesar, after his victory over Pompey, placed her on the Egyptian throne as Queen.—*Caesar and Cleopatra.*

CLEOPATRA-SEMIRAMIS. Old-style woman created by Pygmalion, 31,920 A.D. Wife of Ozymandias.—*Back to Methuselah* ('As Far As Thought Can Reach').

COKANE, WILLIAM DE BURGH. Friend of Harry Trench and later secretary to Lickcheese. 'An ill-nourished, scantily-haired gentleman, with affected manners.'—*Widowers' Houses*.

COLLINS, MRS. GEORGE (ZENOBIA). Mayoress and coal merchant's wife. 'In an historical museum she would explain Edward IV's taste for shopkeepers' wives ... But her beauty is wrecked, like an ageless landscape ravaged by long and fierce war ... The whole face is a battlefield of the passions, quite deplorable until she speaks when an an alert sense of fun rejuvenates her in a moment, and makes her irresistible.'—*Getting Married*.

COLLINS, WILLIAM. Greengrocer and Alderman. 'A reassuring man, with ... the power of saying anything he likes to you without offence.'—*Getting Married*.

COMMISSAR, THE. Bolshevik complainant to the League of Nations about British subversion within Russia. 'A very smart Russian gentleman.'—*Geneva*.

COMMISSIONER. A Diet Commissioner, dictating a primer on past civilisations and their diet.—*Farfetched Fables* (Fourth Fable).

CONFUCIUS. Chief Secretary to the President of the British Islands, 2170 A.D. Virtual controller of affairs of state. 'A man in a yellow gown, presenting the general appearance of a Chinese sage.'—*Back to Methuselah* ('The Thing Happens').

COURCELLES, MASTER DE. Canon of Paris. Young priest associated with indictment of Joan on 64 counts.—*Saint Joan.*

CRAMPTON, FERGUS. Long-absent husband of Mrs. Clandon and father of Gloria and the twins. 'A man about 60, with an atrociously obstinate ill-tempered grasping mouth, and a dogmatic voice.'—*You Never Can Tell.*

CRASSUS. Colonial Secretary. 'Elderly and anxious.'— *The Apple Cart.*

CRAVEN, COL. DANIEL. Julia's father. 'Affects the bluff, simple veteran, and carries it off pleasantly and well . . . a goodnaturedly impulsive credulous person.'—*The Philanderer.*

CRAVEN, JULIA. One of the young women disputing for Charteris's favours. 'As much a study of jealousy as Leontes in *The Winter's Tale.*'—*The Philanderer.*

CRAVEN, SYLVIA. Julia's younger sister, member of the Ibsen Club. 'A pretty girl of 18, small and trim.'—*The Philanderer.*

CROFTS, SIR GEORGE. Mrs. Warren's partner in her 'profession'. 'Gentlemanly combination of the most brutal types of city man, sporting man and man about town.'— *Mrs. Warren's Profession.*

CULLEN, SIR PATRICK. Veteran Irish doctor. 'His manner to Ridgeon, whom he likes, is whimsical and fatherly: to others he is a little gruff and uninviting.'—*The Doctor's Dilemma.*

CUSINS, ADOLPHUS. Major Barbara's fiancé, a Professor of Greek: 'His sense of humour is intellectual and subtle . . . The lifelong struggle of a benevolent temperament and a high conscience against impulses of inhuman ridicule and fierce impatience has set up a chronic strain which has visibly wrecked his constitution.'—*Major Barbara.*

CUTHBERTSON, JOSEPH. Grace Tranfield's father, a dramatic critic. 'A man of fervent idealistic sentiment, so frequently outraged by the facts of life that he has acquired an habitually indignant manner.'—*The Philanderer.*

DANBY. Secretary at Bond Street Picture Gallery.— *The Doctor's Dilemma.*

DANIELS, ELDER. Blanco Posnet's brother, anxious to conceal the fact; a hypocritical ex-drunkard.—*The Shewing-up of Blanco Posnet.*

DASHKOFF, PRINCESS. Lady in waiting to Catherine the Great.—*Great Catherine.*

DAUPHIN, THE (CHARLES VII of France, 'Charles the Victorious', 1422–61). Crowned in Rheims Cathedral after Joan of Arc's victory at Orleans, partly to quell doubts as to his legitimacy. 'He has little narrow eyes, near together, a long pendulous nose . . . and the expression of a young dog accustomed to be kicked, yet incorrigible and irrepressible.'—*Saint Joan.*

DEACONESS, THE. A woman of a sect devoted to Jesus. 'An attractive and very voluble middleaged English lady.' —*Geneva.*

DELANEY, DORA. 'A young lady of hilarious disposition, very tolerable good looks, and killing clothes.'—*Fanny's First Play.*

DEMPSEY, FATHER. 'A priest neither by vocation nor ambition, but because the life suits him.'—*John Bull's Other Island.*

D'ESTIVET, CANON JOHN. Historical character. Promoter at Joan's trial. 'Wellmannered, but vulpine beneath his veneer.'—*Saint Joan.*

DEVIL, THE. Mephistopheles or Lucifer (resembles Mendoza).—*Man and Superman* ('Don Juan in Hell').

DOCTOR. Lord Reginald Fitzambey's physician.—*Musiccure.*

DOCTOR. Young physician to the Patient.—*Too True To Be Good.*

DOMESDAY, DUKE OF. 'An elderly delicately built aristocrat.'—*On the Rocks.*

DOÑA ANA DE ULLOA. Character from Mozart's *Don Giovanni* (resembles Ann Whitefield).—*Man and Superman* ('Don Juan in Hell').

DON JUAN TENORIO. Character from Mozart's *Don Giovanni*, ancestor of John Tanner.—*Man and Superman* ('Don Juan in Hell').

DONKIN, ARCHDEACON DAFFODIL. Prelate angry at his daughter Ermyntrude's extravagance.—*The Inca of Perusalem.*

DOOLITTLE, ALFRED. Eliza's father, a dustman and independent moralistic spokesman for the 'undeserving poor.' —*Pygmalion.*

DOOLITTLE, ELIZA. Flower-girl transformed by Professor Higgins to pass as a duchess.—*Pygmalion*.

DORAN, BARNEY. 'Of sanguine temperament, with an enormous capacity for derisive, obscene, blasphemous, or merely cruel and senseless fun.'—*John Bull's Other Island*.

DOYLE, CORNELIUS. Father of Larry.—*John Bull's Other Island*.

DOYLE, LAURENCE. Civil engineer, partner of Broadbent. 'A man of 36 . . . with a suggestion of thinskinnedness and dissatisfaction that contrasts strongly with Broadbent's eupeptic jollity.'—*John Bull's Other Island*.

DRINKWATER, FELIX ('BRANDYFACED JACK'). One of Brassbound's escorts, a Cockney. 'He is dressed in somebody else's very second best as a coastguardsman, and gives himself the airs of a stage tar.'—*Captain Brassbound's Conversion*.

DRISCOLL, TERESA. Irish parlour-maid, a go-getter once loved by Private O'Flaherty.—*O'Flaherty, V.C.*

DUBEDAT, JENNIFER. Beautiful, idealising Cornish wife of the artist, Louis Dubedat. 'She has something of the grace and romance of a wild creature, with a good deal of the elegance and dignity of a fine lady.'—*The Doctor's Dilemma*.

DUBEDAT, LOUIS. 23-year-old artist of genius, dying of consumption and unscrupulous in everything except his art. 'He is all nerves, and very observant and quick of apprehension . . .'—*The Doctor's Dilemma*.

DUDGEON, CHRISTY. Young brother of Dick. 'Fattish, stupid, fair-haired.'—*The Devil's Disciple*.

DUDGEON, MRS. Mother of Dick. 'Mrs. Dudgeon's face, even at its best, is grimly trenched by the channels into which the barren forms and observances of a dead Puritanism can pen a bitter temper and a fierce pride.'—*The Devil's Disciple*.

DUDGEON, RICHARD (DICK). 'The Devil's Disciple': reprobate of the family, in revolt against false puritanism, and a supporter of American Independence. 'He is certainly the best looking member of the family, but his expression is reckless and sardonic, his manner defiant and satirical, his dress picturesquely careless. Only, his forehead and mouth betray an extraordinary steadfastness, and his eyes are the eyes of a fanatic.'—*The Devil's Disciple*.

DUDGEON, 'UNCLE TITUS'. 'A wiry little terrier of a man . . . the lady's man of the family.'—*The Devil's Disciple*.

DUDGEON, 'UNCLE WILLIAM'. 'A large, shapeless man, bottle-nosed and evidently no ascetic at table.'—*The Devil's Disciple*.

DUNN, BILLY. Burglar, ex-pirate and drunken boatswain of Captain Shotover. No relation to Ellie and Mazzini. Husband of Nurse Guinness. 'An old and villainous-looking man.'—*Heartbreak House*.

DUNN, ELLIE. Young girl disillusioned in romantic love but of strengthening character. 'A pretty girl, slender, fair and intelligent looking.'—*Heartbreak House*.

DUNN, MAZZINI. A good but unsuccessful man; Ellie's father. 'A little elderly man with bulging credulous eyes and earnest manners.'—*Heartbreak House*.

DUNOIS, CAPTAIN JEAN ('BASTARD OF ORLEANS'). Historical character (1402–68), illegitimate first cousin of the Dauphin and one of France's most brilliant soldiers, who fought with Joan of Arc at Orleans. In Shaw, the character is derived also from, and amalgamated with, the Duc D'Alençon, another of Joan's companions at arms. He is Joan's best friend.—*Saint Joan*.

DUVALLET, LIEUTENANT. Frenchman visiting England. 'A goodlooking young marine officer.'—*Fanny's First Play*.

ECRASIA. A girl art critic, eight months old, 31,920 A.D.— *Back to Methuselah* ('As Far As Thought Can Reach').

EDITOR, THE. Man in charge of the gladiators.—*Androcles and the Lion*.

EDSTASTON, CAPTAIN CHARLES. Young English officer of the Light Dragoons who captivates Catherine the Great. 'He is evidently on fairly good terms with himself.'— *Great Catherine*.

EDWARD III, King of England (1312–77). Aged 35. A tempestuous warrior devoted to his Queen.—*The Six of Calais*.

EGYPTIAN DOCTOR. Engaged in work for the English poor, he marries Epifania Fitzfassenden for love of her pulse. 'A serious looking middleaged Egyptian gentleman in an old black frock coat and a tarboosh, speaking English too well to be mistaken for a native.'—*The Millionairess*.

ELDER, THE. Atheistic father of the Burglar. 'A very tall, gaunt elder, by his dress and bearing a well-to-do English gentleman . . . He is in the deepest mourning and his attitude is one of hopeless dejection.'—*Too True To Be Good*.

ELDERLY GENTLEMAN, THE (BLUEBIN BARLOW, O.M.). British Commonwealth visitor to the long-livers' temple in Galway Bay, 3000 A.D. President of the Travellers' Club, Baghdad. A representative of old-fashioned British moral standards and institutions, a short-liver discouraged by his surroundings.—*Back to Methuselah* ('Tragedy of an Elderly Gentleman').

ELIZABETH I, Queen of England (1533–1603). A monarch at first outraged by, then sympathetic to, Shakespeare and his plea for a National Theatre.—*The Dark Lady of the Sonnets*.

EMMY. Sir Colenso Ridgeon's servant.—*The Doctor's Dilemma*.

EMPEROR, THE. Roman Caesar converted to Christianity by the feats of Ferrovius in the arena and Androcles' 'miracle' with the lion. 'Has no sense of the value of common people's lives, and amuses himself with killing as carelessly as with sparing . . .'—*Androcles and the Lion*.

ENVOY'S DAUGHTER. Visitor to the Oracle, 3000 A.D.— *Back to Methuselah* ('Tragedy of an Elderly Gentleman').

ENVOY'S WIFE. Visitor to the Oracle, 3000 A.D.—*Back to Methuselah* ('Tragedy of an Elderly Gentleman').

ERMYNTRUDE. Extravagant widow of a millionaire, daughter of Archdeacon Donkin.—*The Inca of Perusalem*.

ESSIE. Cowed and bullied orphan, an illegitimate Dudgeon child, aged 16. 'A wild, timid looking creature with black hair and tanned skin.'—*The Devil's Disciple*.

EVANS, FEEMY. Prostitute in the wild west. 'A young woman of 23 or 24, with impudent manners, battered good looks, and dirty-fine dress.'—*The Shewing-up of Blanco Posnet*.

EVE. Biblical character, Adam's wife, learning the secret of the creation of life and human survival.—*Back to Methuselah* ('In the Beginning').

EXECUTIONER. Master Executioner of Rouen, who supervised the burning of Joan of Arc.—*Saint Joan*.

EYNSFORD HILL, CLARA. Sister of Freddy. 'A gay air of being very much at home in society, the bravado of genteel poverty.'—*Pygmalion*.

EYNSFORD HILL, FREDDY. Young admirer of Eliza Doolittle (and, according to a later 'postscript' by Shaw, the man she eventually married).—*Pygmalion*.

EYNSFORD HILL, MRS. Their mother. 'Well-bred, quiet, and has the habitual anxiety of straitened means.'—*Pygmalion*.

FAIRMILE, TODGER. Salvation Army sergeant for whom Bill Walker's girl deserts him, he is more than a match for the vengeful Bill: 'E called me Braddher, an dahned me as if Aw was a kid and e was me mather worshin me a Setterda nawt.'—*Major Barbara*.

FANSHAWE, LADY CORINTHIA, President of Anti-Suffragette League. 'Known in musical circles as the Richmond Park nightingale.'—*Press Cuttings*.

FARRELL, MRS. 'A lean, highly respectable charwoman of about 50', later engaged to be married to General Mitchener.—*Press Cuttings.*

FARRELL, PATSY. Superstitious, ill-paid Irish labourer.—*John Bull's Other Island.*

FARWATERS, LADY. Wife of the Governor.—*The Simpleton of the Unexpected Isles.*

FARWATERS, SIR CHARLES. Governor of the Isles.—*The Simpleton of the Unexpected Isles.*

FERROVIUS. Christian of war-like impulses. 'A man whose sensibilities are keen and violent to the verge of madness.' —*Androcles and the Lion.*

FERRUCCIO, COUNT. A young 15th-century Italian nobleman.—*The Glimpse of Reality.*

FIELDING, SERGEANT (THE SERGEANT). Philosophising reader of the *Pilgrim's Progress* and the Bible, attracted to 'Sweetie'. 'A wellbuilt handsome man, getting on for 40.'—*Too True To Be Good.*

FITTON, MARY. The 'Dark Lady' of the Shakespearean sonnets; jealous when finding him with Queen Elizabeth.—*The Dark Lady of the Sonnets.*

FITZAMBEY, LORD REGINALD. Young War Office official suffering a nervous breakdown.—*Music-cure.*

FITZFASSENDEN, ALISTAIR. Epifania's husband. 'A splendid athlete, with most of his brains in his muscles.'—*The Millionairess.*

FITZFASSENDEN, EPIFANIA. The millionairess.—*The Millionairess.*

FITZTOLLEMACHE ('FITZ'). Jealous husband of Lady Magnesia. 'A saturnine figure in evening dress, partially concealed by a crimson cloak.'—*Passion, Poison and Petrifaction.*

FITZTOLLEMACHE, LADY MAGNESIA. Our heroine.—*Passion, Poison and Petrifaction.*

FLANCO DE FORTINBRAS, GENERAL. A dictator risen to power by civil war. 'A middle-aged officer, very smart, and quite conventional.'—*Geneva.*

FLOPPER, SIR FERDINAND. Middle-aged solicitor of Bill Buoyant, billionaire.—*Buoyant Billions.*

FOX, GEORGE. Historical character (1624–1691). Religious and social reformer, founder of the Society of Friends (i.e. the Quakers): known as 'the man in the leather breeches'. 'A big man with bright eyes and a powerful voice in reserve, aged 56.'—*In Good King Charles's Golden Days.*

FRASER, HONORIA. Vivie Warren's lawyer friend, in whose Chancery Lane chambers the fourth act takes place, though she does not appear.—*Mrs. Warren's Profession.*

FTATATEETA. Nurse to Cleopatra; a fierce guardian ready to kill.—*Caesar and Cleopatra.*

FUSIMA. A long-liver 'secondary' (i.e. in her second century), 3000 A.D. 'Her age cannot be guessed; her face is firm and chiselled like a young face; but her expression is unyouthful in its severity and determination.'—*Back to Methuselah* ('Tragedy of an Elderly Gentleman').

GARDNER, FRANK. Rector's son, attracted by Vivie Warren. 'Smartly dressed, cleverly good-for-nothing, not long turned 20, with a charming voice and agreeably disrespectful manners.'—*Mrs. Warren's Profession.*

GARDNER, REV. SAMUEL. Frank's father and ex-lover of Mrs. Warren. 'That obsolescent social phenomenon, the fool of the family dumped on the Church by his father the patron, clamorously asserting himself as father and clergyman without being able to command respect in either capacity.'—*Mrs. Warren's Profession.*

GARNETT, PROSERPINE ('PROSSY'). The Rev. Morell's secretary, in love with him. 'A brisk little woman of about 30, of the lower middle class.'—*Candida.*

GENTLEMAN. A senior on the staff of the Anthropometric Lab.—*Farfetched Fables* (Third Fable).

GEORGE, MRS. Mayoress, loved in his youth by St. John Hotchkiss. 'Every inch a Mayoress in point of stylish dressing . . . she proclaims herself to the first glance as the triumphant, pampered, wilful, intensely alive woman who has always been rich among poor people.'—*Getting Married.*

GILBEY, BOBBY. 'A pretty youth, of very suburban gentility, strong and manly enough by nature but untrained and unsatisfactory . . .'—*Fanny's First Play.*

GILBEY, MRS. Mother of Bobby. 'A placid person.'—*Fanny's First Play.*

GILBEY, ROBIN. Father of Bobby. 'Not at all placid.'—*Fanny's First Play.*

GIRL. A junior on the staff of the Anthropometric Lab.— *Farfetched Fables* (Third Fable).

GISBORNE, ADELAIDE. Cashel Byron's mother, an actress. —*The Admirable Bashville*.

GIULIA. Daughter of an innkeeper, Squarcio.—*The Glimpse of Reality*.

GIUSEPPE. Landlord of the inn at Tavazzano. 'A swarthy vivacious shrewdly cheerful black-curled bullet headed grinning little innkeeper of 40. Naturally an excellent host.'—*The Man of Destiny*.

GLENMORISON. President of the Board of Trade, a Scot.— *On the Rocks*.

GRANTHAM, LESBIA. Unmarried sister of Mrs. Bridgenorth. 'I'm a regular old maid. I'm very particular about my belongings. I like to have my own house, and to have it to myself . . . I am proud of my independence and jealous for it. I have a sufficiently well-stocked mind to be very good company for myself if I have plenty of books and music.'—*Getting Married*.

GUINNESS, NURSE. Indulged servant of Captain Shotover and Hesione Hushabye.—*Heartbreak House*.

GUNN. Critic of 30.—*Fanny's First Play*.

GUNNER. Name given by John Tarleton to Julius Baker, young gunman who threatens to shoot him. Tarleton's natural son, a clerk.—*Misalliance*.

GWYNN, NELL (ELEANOR). Historical character (1650–87). 'Pretty witty Nelly', warm-hearted actress-mistress of Charles II.—*In Good King Charles's Golden Days*.

HAFFIGAN, MATTHEW. Irish farmer.—*John Bull's Other Island*.

HAFFIGAN, TIM. 'Might be a tenth-rate schoolmaster ruined by drink . . . a show of reckless geniality and high spirits, helped out by a rollicking stage brogue.'—*John Bull's Other Island*.

HALLAM, SIR HOWARD. English tourist in Morocco, brother-in-law to Lady Cecily. A lawyer. 'More than elderly, facing old age on compulsion, not resignedly.'—*Captain Brassbound's Conversion*.

HAMMINGTAP, 'IDDY'. The Simpleton of the title. A young English clergyman. 'He has a baby complexion, and a childish expression, credulous and disarmingly propitiatory.'—*The Simpleton of the Unexpected Isles*.

HANNAH. 'Elderly and wise.'—*The Shewing-up of Blanco Posnet*.

HANWAYS, HILDA. Secretary to the Prime Minister.—*On the Rocks*.

HASLAM, REV. WILLIAM ('BILL'). Young rector, later married to 'Savvy' Barnabas. 'Has nothing clerical about him except his collar . . . smiles with a frank schoolboyishness that makes it impossible to be unkind to him.'—*Back to Methuselah* ('The Gospel of the Brothers Barnabas'). (In the later play, 'The Thing Happens', he is the Archbishop of York (*q.v.*).)

HAWKINS, LAWYER. Lawyer to the Dudgeon family, 'looking as much squire as solicitor'.—*The Devil's Disciple*.

HE-ANCIENT. Long-liver of some 800 years, 31,920 A.D. 'In physical hardihood and uprightness he seems to be in the prime of life; and his eyes and mouth show no signs of age; but his face, though fully and firmly fleshed, bears a network of lines . . . His head is finely domed and utterly bald.'—*Back to Methuselah* ('As Far as Thought Can Reach').

HERMAPHRODITE. A hermaphrodite on the staff of the Genetic Institute.—*Farfetched Fables* (Fifth Fable).

HIGGINS, HENRY. Professor of phonetics. 'A robust, vital, appetizing sort of man of 40 or thereabouts . . . rather like a very impetuous baby "taking notice" eagerly and loudly . . . His manner varies from genial bullying when he is in a good humor to stormy petulance when anything goes wrong.'—*Pygmalion*.

HIGGINS, MRS. Professor Higgins's mother.—*Pygmalion*.

HIGHCASTLE, LORD AUGUSTUS. 'A distinguished member of the governing class' in World War I.—*Augustus Does His Bit*.

HILL, JENNY. 'A pale, overwrought, pretty Salvation lass of 18.'—*Major Barbara*.

HIPNEY, OLD. Elderly socialist on his 12th unemployed deputation. 'A sunny comfortable old chap in his Sunday best.'—*On the Rocks*.

HODSON. 'A respectable valet, old enough to have lost all alacrity and acquired an air of putting up patiently with a great deal of trouble . . .'—*John Bull's Other Island*.

HOTCHKISS, ST. JOHN. Intended new husband of Leo Bridgenorth. 'He talks about himself with energetic gaiety. He talks to other people with a sweet forbearance (implying a kindly consideration for their stupidity) which infuriates those whom he does not succeed in amusing.'— *Getting Married.*

HOTSPOT, ADMIRAL SIR BEMROSE. 'A half witted admiral; but the half that has not been sacrificed to his profession is sound and vigorous.'—*On the Rocks.*

HUMPHRIES, TOM (MAYOR of the Isle of Cats).—*On the Rocks.*

HUSHABYE, HECTOR. Hesione's husband, a habitual romantic liar, attractive to women.—*Heartbreak House.*

HUSHABYE, HESIONE. Daughter of Captain Shotover and wife of Hector Hushabye. 'She has magnificent black hair, eyes like fishpools of Heshbon . . .'—*Heartbreak House.*

HYERING, HUGO. Young emigration officer who becomes political secretary to the Isles.—*Simpleton of the Unexpected Isles.*

HYERING, MRS. Young woman immigrant who marries the emigration officer, Hugo.—*The Simpleton of the Unexpected Isles.*

INCA OF PERUSALEM, THE. A burlesque of Kaiser Wilhelm II.—*The Inca of Perusalem.*

INQUISITOR, THE (BROTHER JOHN LEMAÎTRE OF THE ORDER OF ST. DOMINIC). Historical character, actually a deputy for the Chief Inquisitor investigating heresy in

France. A principal at Joan's trial. In Shaw, a 'mild elderly gentleman' with 'evident reserves of authority and firmness', but loquacious on the evils of heresy.—*Saint Joan.*

IRAS. Historical character. Favourite servant to Cleopatra. 'A plump, goodnatured creature, rather fatuous.'— *Caesar and Cleopatra.*

JAMES, DUKE OF YORK (later JAMES II) (1633–1701). Lord High Admiral of England, 1660. A bigoted Catholic viewed with affection but some concern for his future by his brother, Charles II.—*In Good King Charles's Golden Days.*

JANGA. One of the four beautiful eugenic East/West children, brother of Maya and Vashti.—*Simpleton of the Unexpected Isles.*

JEMIMA. The Queen, a 'cabbage' to Orinthia's 'rose', but one who retains the King's devotion.—*The Apple Cart.*

JESSIE. 'A goodnatured but sharptongued, hoity toity young woman.'—*The Shewing-up of Blanco Posnet.*

JEW, THE. Accuser of Battler, the dictator. 'A middle-aged gentleman of distinguished appearance, with a blond beard and moustache, top hatted, frock coated and gloved.'— *Geneva.*

JOAN (JEANNE D'ARC) 1412–31. Not, as Shaw rightly points out, a peasant but the daughter of a farmer of some position in his village, Domrémy.—*Saint Joan.*

JOHN OF GAUNT (1340–99). One of King Edward III's younger sons, aged seven.—*The Six of Calais.*

JOHNSON. One of Brassbound's escort. 'A blackbearded' thickset, slow, middleaged man with an air of damaged respectability.—*Captain Brassbound's Conversion.*

JUDGE, THE. Presiding Judge of International Court at the Hague. 'He is a Dutchman, much younger than a British judge: under 40, in fact, but very grave and every inch a judge.'—*Geneva.*

JUGGINS. Footman to the Gilbeys, secretly brother of a Duke. 'A rather low-spirited man of 35 or more, of good appearance and address, and iron self-command.—*Fanny's First Play.*

JUNO, MRS. Young wife flirting with Gregory Lunn.— *Overruled.*

JUNO, SIBTHORPE. Mrs. Juno's husband, flirting with Mrs. Lunn. 'A fussily energetic little man, who gives himself an air of gallantry by greasing the points of his moustaches.' —*Overruled.*

KANCHIN. One of the four beautiful eugenic East/West children, brother of Maya and Vashti.—*The Simpleton of the Unexpected Isles.*

KEARNEY, CAPTAIN HAMLIN, U.S. Navy. Commander of the cruiser, *Santiago.* 'A robustly built western American . . . A curious ethnological specimen, with all the nations of the old world at war in his veins.'—*Captain Brassbound's Conversion.*

KEEGAN, 'FATHER'. Irish ex-priest, believed mad, but only disillusioned and imaginative. 'With the face of a young saint, yet with white hair and perhaps 50 years on his back.'—*John Bull's Other Island.*

KEMP, SHERIFF. A sheriff in wildwest territory, who makes some attempt at justice and controlling hanging-fever in court.—*The Shewing-up of Blanco Posnet.*

KEMP, STRAPPER. The Sheriff's brother.—*The Shewing-up of Blanco Posnet.*

KÉROUALLE, LOUISE DE ('MRS. CARWELL'), Duchess of Portsmouth. Historical character, 1649–1734. A 'baby-faced' Breton hated in England as the 'French spy', because she helped to arrange Charles's secret financial subsidy from King Louis XIV of France and the sale of Dunkirk to the French. Charles II's mistress.—*In Good King Charles's Golden Days.*

KNELLER, SIR GODFREY. Historical character (1646–1723). Dutch portrait painter, pupil of Rembrandt, who came to London 1676 and was appointed court painter to Charles II, 1680.—*In Good King Charles's Golden Days.*

KNOX, MARGARET. Fiancée of Bobby Gilbey. 'A strong, springy girl of 18, with large nostrils, an audacious chin, and a gaily resolute manner.'—*Fanny's First Play.*

KNOX, MR. Father of Margaret, and partner of Gilbey. 'A troubled man of 50.'—*Fanny's First Play.*

KNOX, MRS. Mother of Margaret. 'A plain woman, dressed without regard to fashion, with thoughtful eyes and thoughtful ways.'—*Fanny's First Play.*

LADVENU, BROTHER MARTIN. Historical character. 'A young but fine-drawn Dominican', sympathetically helpful (as he sees it) to Joan at her trial. Later (1456) associated with her official rehabilitation.—*Saint Joan.*

LADY (a doctor). A woman in grey, principal of a sanatorium in the Welsh mountains for nervous breakdown cases.—*On the Rocks.*

LADY. Beautiful outwitter of Lord Augustus Highcastle.—*Augustus Does His Bit.*

LA HIRE. Historical character, captain under Joan of Arc. 'A war dog with no court manners and pronounced camp ones.'—*Saint Joan.*

LAVINIA. Roman patrician and Christian about to be martyred. 'A good-looking, resolute young woman . . . a clever and fearless freethinker.'—*Androcles and the Lion.*

LENTULUS. Young Roman courtier. 'A slender, fair-haired epicene.'—*Androcles and the Lion.*

LICKCHEESE. Rent collector for Sartorius, later prosperous in the same line of business, slum landlordism. 'A shabby, needy man . . . a nervous, wiry, pertinacious human terrier.'—*Widowers' Houses.*

LIEUTENANT. 'A tall, chuckle-headed young man of 24 . . . A young man without fear, without reverence . . . hopelessly insusceptible to the Napoleonic or any other idea.'—*Man of Destiny.*

LILITH. Mother of the human species (according to this play), having torn herself in two to create Adam and Eve.—*Back to Methuselah.*

LOMAX, CHARLES ('CHOLLY'). Sarah Undershaft's fiancé. 'A young man about town . . . afflicted with a frivolous sense of humour.'—*Major Barbara.*

LOTTIE. 'A sentimental girl.'—*The Shewing-up of Blanco Posnet.*

LOUKA. The Petkoffs' servant, attractive to Sergius. 'A handsome proud girl . . . so defiant that her servility to Raina is almost insolent.'—*Arms and the Man.*

LUBIN, HENRY HOPKINS. Veteran Liberal Party leader. 'Taking his simple dignity for granted, but wonderfully comfortable and quite self-assured.' A ladies' man.— *Back to Methuselah* ('The Gospel of the Brothers Barnabas').

LUCIAN. Lydia Carew's cousin.—*The Admirable Bashville.*

LUCIUS SEPTIMUS. Roman officer, slayer of Pompey, unapproved by Caesar.—*Caesar and Cleopatra.*

LUNN, GREGORY. Young husband flirting with Mrs. Juno. 'He is rather handsome, and has ventured as far in the direction of poetic dandyism in the arrangement of his hair as any man who is not a professional artist can afford to in England.'—*Overruled.*

LUNN, MRS. SERAPHITA. Gregory's wife. 'A handsome languid woman, with flashing dark eyes and long lashes', over-used to admiration and bored by Juno's advances.— *Overruled.*

LUTESTRING, MRS. Domestic Minister, British Islands, 2170 A.D. Long-liver of 274 years. 'She is a handsome woman, apparently in the prime of life, with elegant, tense, well held up figure, and the walk of a goddess. Her expression and deportment are grave, swift, decisive, awful, unanswerable.'—*Back to Methuselah* ('The Thing Happens'). (In earlier part, 'The Gospel of the Brothers Barnabas', she is the Parlor Maid (*q.v.*).)

LYSISTRATA. Powermistress General. 'A grave lady in academic robes', ex-schoolmistress, with a passionate devotion to her department.—*The Apple Cart.*

MADIGAN, GENERAL SIR PEARCE. Squire of Irish country house, who has known O'Flaherty, v.c., from childhood. —*O'Flaherty, V.C.*

MAGNUS, KING. King of England. 'A tallish studious-looking gentleman of 45 or thereabouts.' Highly intelligent and subtle monarch with a diplomat's tact and penetration. —*The Apple Cart.*

MAJOR BARBARA (See Undershaft, Barbara).—*Major Barbara.*

MALONE, HECTOR, Junior. American secretly married to Violet Robinson. 'He is not at all ashamed of his nationality. This makes English people of fashion think well of him, as of a young fellow who is manly enough to confess to an obvious disadvantage without any attempt to conceal or extenuate it.'—*Man and Superman.*

MALONE, HECTOR, Senior. Father of above. Self-made millionaire, an Irish American. 'A man whose social position needs constant and scrupulous affirmation.'—*Man and Superman.*

MANGAN, ALFRED ('BOSS'). Successful businessman and millionaire. 'About 55, with a careworn, mistrustful expression, standing a little on an entirely imaginary dignity.'—*Heartbreak House.*

MARCHBANKS, EUGENE. Poet of aristocratic birth, in love with Candida. 'A strange shy youth of eighteen . . . so uncommon as to be almost unearthly.'—*Candida.*

MARTELLUS. Sculptor, 31,920 A.D. Arjillax's master, who has matured to the point of smashing his statues and preferring life.—*Back to Methuselah* ('As Far As Thought Can Reach').

MARZO. One of Brassbound's escorts. 'An Italian dressed in a much worn suit of serge, a dilapidated Alpine hat, and boots laced with scraps of twine.'—*Captain Brassbound's Conversion.*

MATRON. On the staff of the Anthropometric Lab. 'A comely matron in a purple academic gown.'—*Farfetched Fables* (Third Fable).

MAYA. One of the four beautiful eugenic East/West children: loved by the Simpleton.—*The Simpleton of the Unexpected Isles.*

M'COMAS, FINCH. Solicitor and long-standing friend and legal adviser of Mrs. Clandon.—*You Never Can Tell.*

MEEK, PRIVATE. Military genius who takes command of all army functions, and rides about the desert on a high-powered motor cycle. A private by choice, having resigned three commissions and re-enlisted under new names. —*Too True To Be Good.*

MEGAERA. Androcles' shrewish wife. 'A rather handsome pampered slattern.'—*Androcles and the Lion.*

MELLISH. Cashel Byron's trainer.—*The Admirable Bashville.*

MENDOZA. Bandit chief, ex-waiter, in the Sierra Nevada. 'A tall strong man, with a striking cockatoo nose, glossy black hair, pointed beard, upturned moustache and a

Mephistophelean affection.' (Becomes the Devil in dream interlude, 'Don Juan in Hell'.)—*Man and Superman.*

MERCER. Elderly clerk in the office of the Lord Chancellor.—*The Fascinating Foundling.*

METELLUS. Young Roman courtier. 'Manly—not a talker.'—*Androcles and the Lion.*

MIDLANDER, SIR ORPHEUS. British Foreign Secretary. 'A very well-dressed gentleman of 50 or thereabouts, genial in manner, quickwitted in conversation, altogether a pleasant and popular personality.'—*Geneva.*

MILL, REV. ALEXANDER ('LEXY'). Morell's young curate, a product of Oxford University and 'a conceitedly well intentioned, enthusiastic, immature novice.'—*Candida.*

MITCHENER, GENERAL, of the War Office.—*Press Cuttings.*

MITCHENS, RUMMY. Salvation Army shelter habituée. 'A commonplace old bundle of poverty and hard-worn humanity.'—*Major Barbara.*

MONSTER. An ailing bacillus who claims he has caught measles from the Patient.—*Too True To Be Good.*

MOPPLY, MISS. (See Patient, The.)—*Too True To Be Good.*

MOPPLY, MRS. (The Elderly Lady). The Patient's overfussing mother.—*Too True To Be Good.*

MORELL, REV. JAMES MAVOR. Candida's husband, a Christian Socialist. 'A vigorous, genial, popular man of forty . . . a first-rate clergyman . . . a great baby, pardonably vain of his powers and unconsciously pleased with himself.'—*Candida.*

MORRISON. Butler to Lady Britomart.—*Major Barbara.*

NAPOLEON. Historical character (1769–1821). Aged 27 in Shaw's play, not yet Emperor and conducting the Italian campaign. 'He has prodigious powers of work, and a clear realistic knowledge of human nature in public affairs . . . He is imaginative without illusions, and creative without religion, loyalty, patriotism or any of the common ideals.' —*Man of Destiny.*

NAPOLEON. (AUFSTEIG, GENERAL, *q.v.*). A General, 3000 A.D.—*Back to Methuselah* ('Tragedy of an Elderly Gentleman').

NARYSHKIN. Chamberlain to Catherine the Great.— *Great Catherine.*

NATIVE, THE. Sophisticated philosophic native servant employed by Clementina Buoyant.—*Buoyant Billions.*

NEGRESS. Minister of Health, British Islands, 2170 A.D. A handsome Negress attractive to Burge-Lubin: seen and heard only on the television-telephone.—*Back to Methuselah* ('The Thing Happens').

NEWCOMER. Accuser of Bombardone the dictator. 'An obstinate-looking middle-aged man of respectable but not aristocratic appearance.'—*Geneva.*

NEWTON, SIR ISAAC. Historical character (1642–1727). Great natural philosopher and discoverer of law of gravitation. In Shaw, an absent-minded, peppery mathematician putting more value on his study of the chronology of the Scriptures than his science.—*In Good King Charles's Golden Days.*

NICOBAR. Foreign Secretary, 'snaky and censorious'.— *The Apple Cart.*

NICOLA. The Petkoffs' male servant, engaged to Louka. 'A middleaged man of cool temperament and low but clear and keen intelligence.'—*Arms and the Man.*

NURSE. (See Simpkins, Susan)—*Too True To Be Good.*

O'DOWDA, COUNT. A rich aesthete, father of Fanny. 'A handsome man of 50, dressed with studied elegance a hundred years out of date.'—*Fanny's First Play.*

O'DOWDA, FANNY. Young Suffragette author of a first play: daughter of the Count O'Dowda.—*Fanny's First Play.*

O'FLAHERTY, MRS. Mother of Dennis O'Flaherty, v.c., vociferously pro-Irish.—*O'Flaherty, V.C.*

O'FLAHERTY, PRIVATE DENNIS. Young Irish soldier who has won the Victoria Cross in World War I, and acquired a new insight into the nature of war and human beings.—*O'Flaherty, V.C.*

OLDHAND, LORD. Of the Foreign Office.—*Farfetched Fables* (Second Fable).

ORACLE, THE (also known as The PYTHONESS). Oracle of the temple, Galway, 3000 A.D. A long-liver, aged 170

years. 'A veiled and robed woman of majestic carriage.'—
Back to Methuselah ('Tragedy of an Elderly Gentleman').

ORDERLY. In the War Office. 'An unsoldierly, slovenly,
discontented young man.'—*Press Cuttings*.

ORINTHIA. The King's mistress, fascinating, ambitious
and devious.—*The Apple Cart*.

OSMAN ALI. 'A tall, skinny, whiteclad, elderly Moor.'—
Captain Brassbound's Conversion.

OUDEBOLLE, GILLES D'. Historical character. One of the
six burghers.—*The Six of Calais*.

OZYMANDIAS. Old-style man created by Pygmalion,
31,920 A.D. Calls himself 'King of Kings', quoting Shelley's
sonnet.—*Back to Methuselah* ('As Far as Thought Can
Reach').

PAMPHILIUS. One of the King's private secretaries.
Middle-aged.—*The Apple Cart*.

PANDRANATH, SIR JAFNA. 'An elderly Cingalese pluto-
crat, small and slender to the verge of emaciation, ele-
gantly dressed, but otherwise evidently too much occupied
and worried by making money to get any fun out of
spending it.'—*On the Rocks*.

PARADISE, WILLIAM. Cashel Byron's boxing opponent.—
The Admirable Bashville.

PARAMORE, DR. A vivisectionist. 'Cultivates the professional bedside manner with scrupulous conventionality.'—
The Philanderer.

PARLOR MAID. Young working-class woman about to get married: employed by Franklyn Barnabas.—*Back to Methuselah* ('The Gospel of the Brothers Barnabas'). (In later part, 'The Thing Happens', LUTESTRING, MRS., *q.v.*)

PATIENT ('MOPS', or MISS MOPPLY): Naturally vigorous young woman who breaks free of illness induced by luxurious cosseting, and runs away with the Burglar.— *Too True To Be Good.*

PATIOMKIN (Shavian spelling of POTEMKIN), GREGORY ALEXANDROVITCH. Historical character, 1739–1791. Favourite and able minister of Catherine the Great. 'Gigantic in stature and build . . . superficially a violent, brutal barbarian . . . He has a wild sense of humour, which enables him to laugh at himself as well as at everybody else.'— *Great Catherine.*

PEARCE, MRS. Professor Higgins's housekeeper.—*Pygmalion.*

PERCIVAL, JOEY. An aviator, Bentley's friend and ultimately Hypatia's new fiancé.—*Misalliance.*

PETKOFF, CATHERINE. Mother of Raina. 'Imperiously energetic, with magnificent black hair and eyes, who might be a very splendid specimen of the wife of a mountain farmer, but is determined to be a Viennese lady, and to that end wears a fashionable tea gown on all occasions.'— *Arms and the Man.*

PETKOFF, MAJOR PAUL. Raina's father: 'a cheerful, excitable, insignificant, unpolished man of about 50 . . . greatly pleased with the military rank which the war has thrust upon him.'—*Arms and the Man.*

PETKOFF, RAINA. Romantic young Bulgarian lady of wealth and social pretensions.—*Arms and the Man.*

PHILIPPA OF HAINAULT, QUEEN OF KING EDWARD III (1314–1369). Aged 33. *Enceinte,* loving and merciful, as in history.—*The Six of Calais.*

PHYLLIS. Maid to Lady Magnesia.—*Passion, Poison and Petrifaction.*

PICKERING, COLONEL. Friend of Professor Higgins and author of *Spoken Sanscrit.* 'An elderly gentleman of amiable military type.'—*Pygmalion.*

PLINY. Chancellor of the Exchequer, 'goodhumored and conciliatory.'—*The Apple Cart.*

POSNET, BLANCO. Blasphemous and derisive of wild west values: accused of stealing a horse. 'Evidently a blackguard.'—*The Shewing-up of Blanco Posnet.*

POTHINUS. Historical character. Guardian to Ptolemy, boy king of Egypt. 'A eunuch, passionate, energetic and quick witted, but of common mind and character.'—*Caesar and Cleopatra.*

POULENGEY, BERTRAND DE. Historical character, a gentleman-at-arms, aged 36, who accompanied Joan of Arc to the Dauphin.—*Saint Joan.*

PRA. Handsome native priest.—*The Simpleton of the Unexpected Isles.*

PRAED ('PRADDY'). Architect, old friend but not a lover of Mrs. Warren. 'Hardly past middle age, with something of the artist about him.'—*Mrs. Warren's Profession.*

PRICE, 'SNOBBY'. Salvation Army shelter layabout. 'Young, agile, a talker, a poser, sharp enough to be capable of anything in reason except honesty and altruistic considerations of any kind.'—*Major Barbara*.

PRIEST, THE: of Chinese temple in Belgrave Square home of Bill Buoyant.—*Buoyant Billions*.

PRINCESS, THE. Nervous spinster about to be engaged to a son of the Inca.—*The Inca of Perusalem*.

PROLA. Handsome native priestess.—*The Simpleton of the Unexpected Isles*.

PROTEUS, 'JOE'. Prime Minister in Labour Government: an astute politician who knows exactly how to 'place' his tempers to political advantage.—*The Apple Cart*.

PTOLEMY DIONYSUS. Historical character. 10-year-old King of Egypt, Cleopatra's younger brother and, by Egyptian royal tradition, husband. Killed in Alexandrine War.—*Caesar and Cleopatra*.

PYGMALION. Scientist, 31,920 A.D., who creates two old-style human beings, one of whom kills him.—*Back to Methuselah* ('As Far As Thought Can Reach').

RA. God of Egypt, who speaks the Prologue to the play at the Temple of Ra in Memphis. Written by Shaw as an alternative opening, 1912.—*Caesar and Cleopatra*.

RAIS, GILLES DE. Historical character, known as 'Bluebeard' because of beard dyed blue. Later hanged after sensational trial for multiple murder of children. A young aristocrat and patron of the arts, deviser of pageants.

'He is determined to make himself agreeable, but lacks natural joyousness, and is not really pleasant.'—*Saint Joan*.

RAMSDEN, ROEBUCK. Friend of Ann Whitefield's father, made joint-guardian of her in his will. 'He is more than a highly respectable man: he is marked out as a President of highly respectable men.'—*Man and Superman*.

RAMSDEN, MISS SUSAN. Roebuck's sister. 'A hardheaded old maiden lady in a plain brown silk gown, with enough rings, chains, and brooches to show that her plainness of dress is a matter of principle, not poverty.'—*Man and Superman*.

RANKIN, LESLIE. Missionary at Mogador in Morocco. 'An elderly Scotchman, spiritually a little weatherbeaten.'—*Captain Brassbound's Conversion*.

RAPHAEL. A feathered youth, an earth visitant from the world of Disembodied Thoughts.—*Farfetched Fables* (Sixth and Last Fable).

REDBROOK, KIDDY. One of Brassbound's escort. 'A pleasantly worthless young English gentleman gone to the bad.'—*Captain Brassbound's Conversion*.

REDPENNY. Medical student, acting as Sir Colenso Ridgeon's secretary and assistant.—*The Doctor's Dilemma*.

REILLY, NORA. Preferring her former boy-friend, Laurence Doyle, she is persuaded to accept his business partner Thomas Broadbent instead. 'Her comparative delicacy of manner and sensibility of apprehension, her fine hands and frail figure, her novel accent, with the caressing plaintive Irish melody of her speech, give her a charm which is all the more effective because, being untravelled, she is unconscious of it.'—*John Bull's Other Island.*

RETIARIUS. A gladiator.—*Androcles and the Lion.*

RIDGEON, SIR COLENSO. Eminent doctor recently knighted for the discovery of a method of curing tuberculosis. 'A man of 50 who has never shaken off his youth.'—*The Doctor's Dilemma.*

RIGHTSIDE, SIR DEXTER. Foreign Secretary and a diehard leader of the Conservative Party.—*On the Rocks.*

ROBINSON, OCTAVIUS ('Tavy'). Romantic-minded, unsuccessful young suitor of Ann Whitefield. 'He must, one thinks, be the jeune premier; for it is not in reason to suppose that a second such attractive male figure should appear in one story.'—*Man and Superman.*

ROBINSON, VIOLET. Octavius' sister. 'As impenitent and self-possessed a young lady as one would desire to see . . . a personality which is as formidable as it is exquisitely pretty.'—*Man and Superman.*

ROSE. Woman on the staff of the Genetic Institute, identified by a rose on her tunic.—*Farfetched Fables* (Fifth Fable).

ROSTY, PIERS DE ('HARDMOUTH'). Historical character. One of the six burghers, who defies and taunts King Edward III. 'He has an extraordinarily dogged chin . . . an attitude of intense recalcitrance.'—*The Six of Calais.*

RUFIO. Roman officer, devotedly loyal to Caesar. 'A burly, black-bearded man of middle age, very blunt, prompt and rough.'—*Caesar and Cleopatra.*

SAGAMORE, JULIUS. 'A smart young solicitor.'—*The Millionairess.*

SALLY. Sir Isaac Newton's maid.—*In Good King Charles's Golden Days.*

SANDRO. Young fisherman engaged to Giulia.—*The Glimpse of Reality.*

SANDSTONE, GENERAL. Commander-in-Chief of the British Army.—*Press Cuttings.*

SARANOFF, MAJOR SERGIUS. Raina's fiancé, a sham Byronic hero. 'A tall, romantically handsome man', who has acquired 'the half tragic half ironic air, the mysterious moodiness, the suggestion of a strange and terrible history that has left nothing but undying remorse, by which Childe Harold fascinated the grandmothers of his English contemporaries.'—*Arms and the Man.*

SARTORIUS. Father of Blanche: a wealthy slum landlord. 'A self-made man, formidable to servants, not easily accessible to anyone.'—*Widowers' Houses.*

SARTORIUS, BLANCHE. Daughter of a wealthy slum landlord. 'A well-dressed, well-fed, good-looking, strong-minded young woman, presentably ladylike, but still her father's daughter. Nevertheless fresh and attractive, and none the worse for being vital and energetic rather than delicate and refined.'—*Widowers' Houses.*

SAVOYARD, CECIL. An Impresario. 'A middle-aged man in evening dress and a fur-lined overcoat.'—*Fanny's First Play.*

SCHNEIDEKIND, LIEUTENANT. Subordinate of General Strammfest.—*Annajanska, the Bolshevik Empress.*

SCHUTZMACHER, DR. LEO. A Jewish doctor.—*The Doctor's Dilemma.*

'SECONDBORN'. Bill Buoyant's second son. 'I am a bit of a mathematician.'—*Buoyant Billions.*

'SECONDBORN, MRS.' Wife of Bill Buoyant's second son. 'An aggressive woman.'—*Buoyant Billions.*

SECRETARY OF THE LEAGUE OF NATIONS. 'A disillusioned official . . . One pities him, as he is of a refined type, and, one guesses, began as a Genevan idealist.'—*Geneva.*

SECUTOR. A gladiator.—*Androcles and the Lion.*

SEMPRONIUS. The King's Secretary. 'Smart and still presentably young.'—*The Apple Cart.*

SERGEANT. English soldier sent to arrest Anthony Anderson.—*Devil's Disciple.*

SERPENT, THE. The subtle and wise creature in the Garden of Eden who has learned to speak and teaches Eve the secret of the creation of life.—*Back to Methuselah* ('In the Beginning').

SHAKES. William Shakespeare.—*Shakes Versus Shav.* Shakespeare is also prominent in the *The Dark Lady of the Sonnets.*

SHAMROCK. Man on the staff of the Genetic Institute, identified by a shamrock on his tunic.—*Farfetched Fables* (Fifth Fable).

SHAV. Bernard Shaw.—*Shakes Versus Shav.*

SHE-ANCIENT. Wise long-liver of some 700 years, 31,920 A.D. 'She is like the He-Ancient, equally bald, and equally without sexual charm, but intensely interesting and rather terrifying.'—*Back to Methuselah* ('As Far As Thought Can Reach').

SHIRLEY, PETER. Independent, honest but unemployed, given Salvation Army help and disliking the necessity. 'A half-hardened, half worn-out elderly man, weak with hunger.'—*Major Barbara*.

SHOTOVER, CAPTAIN. Eccentric inventor and ex-seaman. 'An ancient but still hardy man with an immense white beard, in a reefer jacket with a whistle hanging from his neck.'—*Heartbreak House*.

SIDI EL ASSIF, SHEIKH: 'A nobly handsome Arab, hardly thirty.'—*Captain Brassbound's Conversion*.

SIMPKINS, SUSAN ('SWEETIE', or THE NURSE). Pretty, commonsensical, amoral young woman thief, accomplice of The Burglar: later disguised as a Countess.—*Too True To Be Good*.

SMITH. Father of Junius.—*Buoyant Billions*.

SMITH, JUNIUS: In love with Clementina Buoyant. 'In his earliest twenties, smart, but artistically unconventional.'—*Buoyant Billions*.

SMITH, PATRICIA (affectionately known as 'Polly Seedy-stockings'). Beloved by the millionairess's husband.—*The Millionairess*.

SOAMES, OLIVER CROMWELL ('FATHER ANTHONY'). Chaplain to the Bishop of Chelsea; ex-solicitor. 'He is a celibate; fasts strictly on Fridays and throughout Lent; wears a cassock and biretta.'—*Getting Married.*

SOLDIER. Unnamed character who tied together two sticks at Joan's execution to hold up to her as a crucifix. In Shaw's Epilogue, a goodhumoured roisterer given a day a year off from Hell for the deed.—*Saint Joan.*

SPINTHO. A craven thief turned Christian only in hope of eternal life.—*Androcles and the Lion.*

SQUARCIO. Giulia's father, a fifteenth-century Italian inn-keeper.—*The Glimpse of Reality.*

ST. PIERRE, EUSTACHE DE. Historical character. One of the six burghers.—*The Six of Calais.*

STATUE, THE. Ghost in statue form of the Commendatore, Ana's father slain by Don Juan, from Mozart's *Don Giovanni* (resembles Roebuck Ramsden).—*Man and Superman* ('Don Juan in Hell').

STEWARD to Robert de Baudricourt. 'A trodden worm, scanty of flesh, scanty of hair, who might be any age from 18 to 55, being the sort of man whom age cannot wither because he has never bloomed.'—*Saint Joan.*

STOGUMBER, JOHN DE. Chaplain to the Cardinal of Winchester. Virulent opponent of Joan of Arc, satirised for his narrow English patriotism. In the Epilogue a gentle old man, mentally deranged by the shock of seeing Joan burn.—*Saint Joan.*

STRAMMFEST, GENERAL. Cynical commander-in-chief of the Revolutionary forces.—*Annajanska, the Bolshevik Empress.*

STRANGE LADY, THE. A young woman of breeding who steals dispatches in an attempt to prevent Napoleon from reading a private letter. 'She is tall and extraordinarily graceful . . . very feminine, but by no means weak.'— *The Man of Destiny*.

STRAKER, HENRY. Polytechnic-educated chauffeur of John Tanner, called by him 'the New Man'. 'With Tanner and Tanner's friends his manner is not in the least deferential, but cool and reticent . . . Nevertheless, he has a vigilant eye on them always, and that, too, rather cynically, like a man who knows the world well from its seamy side.'— *Man and Superman*.

STREPHON. Youth of two years, 31,920 A.D. In love with Chloe, twice his age, and romantically disconsolate at her desertion.—*Back to Methuselah* ('As Far As Thought Can Reach').

SUMMERHAYS, BENTLEY. A young aristocrat, engaged to Hypatia Tarleton. 'One of those smallish, thinskinned youths, who from 17 to 70 retain unaltered the mental airs of the later and the physical appearance of the earlier age.' —*Misalliance*.

SUMMERHAYS, LORD. Father of Bentley.—*Misalliance*.

SWEETIE (See Simpkins, Susan).—*Too True To Be Good*.

SWINDON, MAJOR. Serving under General Burgoyne and the butt of his sarcasm. 'A pale, sandy-haired, very conscientious-looking man of about 45.'—*The Devil's Disciple*.

SYKES, CECIL. Bridegroom of Edith Bridgenorth. 'A young gentleman with good looks of the serious kind, somewhat careworn by an exacting conscience.'—*Getting Married.*

SZCZEPANOWSKA, LINA. Polish acrobat, strongly independent and 'a remarkably good looking woman'.—*Misalliance.*

TALLBOYS, COLONEL. Commander of British expeditionary force in middle east, with a taste for painting in water colours.—*Too True To Be Good.*

TANNER, JOHN. Author of *The Revolutionists' Handbook*, a bachelor rebel against marriage and the Establishment, defeated by the Life Force. 'Jupiter rather than Apollo. He is prodigiously fluent of speech, restless, excitable . . . possibly a little mad.'—*Man and Superman.*

TARLETON, HYPATIA. Daughter of John. 'Boundless energy and audacity.'—*Misalliance.*

TARLETON, JOHN. 'An immense and genial veteran of trade' (i.e. Tarleton's Underwear): given to quoting literature and still a vital ladies' man.—*Misalliance.*

TARLETON, JOHNNY. Son of John. 'An ordinary young business man.'—*Misalliance.*

TARLETON, MRS. John Tarleton's wife. 'A shrewd and motherly old lady.'—*Misalliance.*

TEACHER. Sixth Form teacher, a matron in cap and gown, in a future atavistic civilisation.—*Farfetched Fables* (Sixth and Last Fable).

THEODOTUS. Tutor to Ptolemy, boy king of Egypt. 'A little old man . . . He maintains an air of magpie keenness and profundity.'—*Caesar and Cleopatra.*

THUNDRIDGE, STREGA. The lady pianist paid by Lord Reginald Fitzambey's mother to cure his nervous trouble. 'I believe Mr. Paderewski has been called the male Thundridge; but no gentleman would dream of repeating such offensive vulgarity.'—*The Music-cure.*

'THIRDBORN, MRS.' Wife of Bill Buoyant's third son. 'Gentle, beautiful, and saintly.'—*Buoyant Billions.*

THISTLE. Man on the staff of the Genetic Institute, identified by a thistle on his tunic.—*Farfetched Fables* (Fifth Fable).

TINWELL, MINNIE. Maid at Star and Garter Hotel, Richmond, once bigamously married to, and deserted by, Dubedat.—*The Doctor's Dilemma.*

TOURIST. 'His embroidered smock and trimmed beard proclaim the would-be artist.'—*Farfetched Fables* (Third Fable).

TRAMP. A genius eventually employed by the Anthropometric Lab. 'A young man in rags.'—*Farfetched Fables* (Third Fable).

TRANFIELD, GRACE. In love with Charteris. 'About 32, slight of build . . . and sensitive in expression . . . but her well closed mouth, proudly set brows, firm chin, and elegant carriage shew plenty of determination and self-respect.'— *The Philanderer.*

TRÉMOUILLE, MONSEIGNEUR DE LA. Historical character, Lord Chamberlain to the Dauphin who owes him money. 'A monstrous arrogant wineskin of a man.'—*Saint Joan.*

TRENCH, DR. HARRY. In love with Blanche Sartorius. An opponent of slum landlordism who compromises on the issue when discovering his own income is involved. 'About 24 . . . with undignified medical-student manners, frank, hasty, rather boyish.'—*Widowers' Houses.*

TROTTER. A critic, affecting a diplomat's dress, with sword and three-cornered hat. Aged about 50.—*Fanny's First Play.*

ULSTERBRIDGE. Commander-in-Chief, War Office.—*Far-fetched Fables* (Second Fable).

UNDERSHAFT, ANDREW. Wealthy armaments manufacturer; Major Barbara's father. 'A stoutish, easygoing elderly man, with kindly patient manners, and an engaging simplicity of character. But he has a watchful, deliberate, waiting, listening face, and formidable reserves of power . . .'—*Major Barbara.*

UNDERSHAFT, BARBARA (MAJOR BARBARA). Andrew Undershaft's daughter. A girl of good family with character enough to join the Salvation Army and work among the poor.—*Major Barbara.*

UNDERSHAFT, LADY BRITOMART. Wife of Andrew Undershaft. 'A very typical managing matron of the upper class.'—*Major Barbara.*

UNDERSHAFT, SARAH. Barbara's sister. 'Slender, bored and mundane.'—*Major Barbara.*

UNDERSHAFT, STEPHEN. Barbara's brother. 'A gravely correct young man under 25, taking himself very seriously.' —*Major Barbara*.

UTTERWORD, LADY (ARIADNE). Daughter of Captain Shotover. 'A woman of the world, by nature in rebellion against the eccentricity of her upbringing.'—*Heartbreak House*.

UTTERWORD, RANDALL. Lady Utterword's brother-in-law, a petulant and useless socialite. 'He has an engaging air of being young and unmarried, but on close inspection is found to be at least over 40.'—*Heartbreak House*.

VALENTINE. A young dentist, in love with Gloria Clandon. 'A thoughtless pleasantry which betrays the young gentleman, still unsettled and in search of amusing adventures.' —*You Never Can Tell*.

VANHATTAN. American Ambassador. 'Mr. Vanhattan enters in an effusive condition, and, like a man assured of an enthusiastic welcome, hurries to the Queen, and salutes her with a handshake so prolonged that she stares in astonishment.'—*The Apple Cart*.

VARINKA. Pretty niece of Potemkin.—*Great Catherine*.

VASHTI. One of the four beautiful eugenic East/West children; Maya's sister.—*The Simpleton of the Unexpected Isles*.

VAUGHAN. Critic of 40.—*Fanny's First Play*.

VILLIERS, BARBARA, Duchess of Cleveland. Historical character (1640–1709). Mistress of Charles II, earlier

made Lady Castlemaine (1661). A jealous termagant.—
In Good King Charles's Golden Days.

VULLIAMY, ANASTASIA. A beautiful foundling.—*The Fascinating Foundling*.

WAGGONER, Jo. An elderly carter.—*The Shewing-up of Blanco Posnet*.

WAITER, THE (See Bohun, Walter).—*You Never Can Tell*.

WALKER, BILL. A bully, threatening and resentful of the Salvation Army's conversion of his girl. 'A rough customer of about 25.'—*Major Barbara*.

WALPOLE, MR. CUTLER. Fashionable surgeon, addicted to removing the 'nuciform sac'. 'He seems never at a loss, never in doubt.'—*The Doctor's Dilemma*.

WARREN, MRS. KITTY. A woman who from economic necessity has made a good living as brothel proprietress. 'Rather spoilt and domineering, and decidedly vulgar, but, on the whole, a genial and fairly presentable old blackguard of a woman.'—*Mrs. Warren's Profession*.

WARREN, VIVIE. Mrs. Warren's daughter, ex-Newnham College, Cambridge. 'An attractive specimen of the sensible, able, highly-educated young middle-class Englishwoman. Age 22. Prompt, strong, confident, self-possessed.'
—*Mrs. Warren's Profession*.

WARWICK, EARL OF, Richard de Beauchamp. Historical character. Tutor of the boy king, Henry VI. In *Saint Joan*, the spokesman for the feudal system, and a political opportunist, advocating the burning of Joan for reasons of policy, not personal dislike or cruelty. 'An imposing nobleman, aged 46.'—*Saint Joan.*

WAYNFLETE, LADY CECILY. English tourist in Morocco. 'Between 30 and 40, tall, very goodlooking, sympathetic, intelligent, tender and humorous . . . A woman of great vitality and humanity.'—*Captain Brassbound's Conversion.*

WHITEFIELD, ANN. John Tanner's pursuer: the embodiment of the Life Force and women's biological urge for procreation. 'Turn up her nose, give a cast to her eye, replace her black and violet confection by the apron and feathers of the flower girl, strike all the aitches out of her speech, and Ann would still make men dream.'—*Man and Superman.*

WHITEFIELD, MRS. Ann's mother. 'She has an expression of muddled shrewdness, a squeak of protest in her voice.'—*Man and Superman.*

WIDOW, THE ('DOLORES'). Self-styled victim of the 'blood feud'. 'A Creole lady of about 40, with the remains of a gorgeous and opulent southern beauty.'—*Geneva.*

'WIDOWER, THE'. Middleaged son of Bill Buoyant.—*Buoyant Billions.*

WILKS. Clerk of emigration office, who commits suicide.—*The Simpleton of the Unexpected Isles.*

WISSANT, DE, JACQUES. Historical character. One of the six burghers.—*The Six of Calais.*

WISSANT, DE, PIERS. Historical character. One of the six burghers.—*The Six of Calais.*

WOMAN. A woman whose child has died and who refuses to identify Blanco as the man who lent her a stolen horse to try and reach a doctor.—*The Shewing-up of Blanco Posnet.*

WORTHINGTON, LORD. Cashel Byron's backer and intended father-in-law.—*The Admirable Bashville.*

YOUNG MAN. Chemist in a chlorine gas factory, later inventor of a new destructive volatile gas.—*Farfetched Fables* (First Fable).

YOUNG WOMAN. Refuses to marry because of war and the atom bomb.—*Farfetched Fables* (First Fable).

'Z'. Talkative young woman on a pleasure cruise, assistant and postmistress in a village grocery store. 'Presentable but not aristocratic.'—*Village Wooing.*

ZOO. 'Nurse' to the Elderly Gentleman, a young (i.e. 56 years old) long-liver, 3000 A.D. 'She looks no older than Savvy Barnabas, whom she somewhat resembles, looked a thousand years before. Younger, if anything.'—*Back to Methuselah* ('Tragedy of an Elderly Gentleman').

ZOZIM. 'Nurse' to the Elderly Gentleman, a first century male long-liver, 3000 A.D.—*Back to Methuselah* ('Tragedy of an Elderly Gentleman').

A SAMPLER OF QUOTATIONS

ON ENGLAND AND THE ENGLISH

'Scratch an Englishman, and find a Protestant.'—Bishop of Beauvais, *Saint Joan*.

'No Englishman is ever fairly beaten.'—de Stogumber, *Saint Joan*.

'Talk to an Englishman about anything serious, and he listens to you curiously for a moment just as he listens to a chap playing classical music. Then he goes back to his marine golf, or motoring, or flying, or women, just like a bit of stretched elastic when you let it go.'—Burge-Lubin, 'The Thing Happens,' *Back to Methuselah*.

'Take care, Ernest. This is part of the British technique. You were talking of something really important. That is dangerous. He switches you off to something of no importance whatever.'—Bombardone, *Geneva*.

'An English crowd will never do anything, mischievous or the reverse, while it is listening to speeches. And the fellows who make the speeches can be depended on never to do anything else.'—Basham, *On the Rocks*.

'Give me English birds and English trees, English dogs and Irish horses, English rivers and English ships; but English men! No, NO, NO.'—Charles II, *In Good King Charles's Golden Days*.

'No one can govern the English: that is why they will never come to any good.'—Catherine of Braganza, *In Good King Charles's Golden Days*.

'God help England if she had no Scots to think for her.'—Proteus, *The Apple Cart*.

'When you find some country gentleman keeping up the old English customs at Christmas and so forth, who is he? An American who has bought the place.'—Vanhattan, *The Apple Cart*.

'There is nothing so bad or so good that you will not find Englishmen doing it; but you will never find an Englishman in the wrong. He does everything on principle.'—Napoleon, *The Man of Destiny*.

Hector: 'And this ship that we are all in? This soul's prison we call England?'

Captain Shotover: 'The captain is in his bunk, drinking bottled ditch-water; and the crew is gambling in the forecastle. She will strike and sink and split. Do you think the laws of God will be suspended in favor of England because you were born in it?'

Hector: 'Well, I dont mean to be drowned like a rat in a trap. I still have the will to live. What am I to do?'

Captain Shotover: 'Do? Nothing simpler. Learn your business as an Englishman.'

Hector: 'And what may my business as an Englishman be, pray?'

Captain Shotover: 'Navigation. Learn it and live; or leave it and be damned.' *Heartbreak House*.

'If a man is known to have been at Oxford or Cambridge nobody ever asks whether he has taken a degree or not.'—Secondborn, *Buoyant Billions*.

'Each pallid English face conceals a brain
Whose powers are proven in the works of Newton
And in the plays of the immortal Shakespear.
There is not one of all the thousands here

But, if you placed him naked in the desert,
Would presently construct a steam engine,
And lay a cable t' th' Antipodes.'
—Lucian, *The Admirable Bashville.*

MANKIND AND SOCIETY

Social questions are produced by the conflict of human institutions with human feeling.—*The Humanitarian*, May 1895.

'I never expect a soldier to think.'—Dick Dudgeon, *The Devil's Disciple.*

The novelties of one generation are only the resuscitated fashions of the generation before last.—Preface to *Three Plays for Puritans.*

All censorships exist to prevent anyone from challenging current conceptions and existing institutions. All progress is initiated by challenging current conceptions, and executed by supplanting existing institutions.—Preface to *Mrs. Warren's Profession.*

The man who cannot see that starvation, overwork, dirt, and disease are as anti-social as prostitution—that they are the vices and crimes of a nation, and not merely its misfortunes—is (to put it as politely as possible) a hopelessly Private Person.—Preface to *Mrs. Warren's Profession.*

The character of Dubedat illustrates one of my pet theses, which is that no man is scrupulous all round. He has, according to his faculties and interests, certain points of honor, whilst in matters that do not interest him he is careless and unscrupulous.—Preface to *The Doctor's Dilemma.*

'A blackguard's a blackguard; an honest man's an honest man; and neither of them will ever be at a loss for a religion or a morality to prove that their ways are the right ways. It's the same with nations, the same with professions, the same all the world over and always will be.'—Sir Patrick Cullen, *The Doctor's Dilemma.*

'But how are we to bear this dreadful new nakedness: the nakedness of the souls who until now have always disguised themselves from one another in beautiful impossible idealisms to enable them to bear one another's company. The iron lightning of war has burnt great rents in these angelic veils, just as it has smashed great holes in our cathedral roofs and torn great gashes in our hillsides. Our souls go in rags now; and the young are spying through the holes and getting glimpses of the reality that was hidden. And they are not horrified; they exult in having found us out . . . we have outgrown our religion, outgrown our political system, outgrown our own strength of mind and character . . .'—The Burglar, *Too True to be Good.*

'I paint pictures to make me feel sane. Dealing with men and women makes me feel mad. Humanity always fails me: Nature never.'—Colonel Tallboys, *Too True to be Good.*

'Naked bodies no longer shock us: our sunbathers, grinning at us from every illustrated summer number of our magazines, are nuder than shorn lambs. But the horror of the naked mind is still more than we can bear.'—The Burglar, *Too True to be Good.*

'I stand midway between youth and age like a man who has missed his train: too late for the last and too early for the next.'—The Burglar, *Too True to be Good.*

People who think they can be honestly free all the time are idiots: people who seek whole-time freedom by putting their share of productive work on others are thieves.— Preface to *Too True to be Good*.

'I am a faith healer. You dont suppose I believe the bottles cure people? But the patient's faith in the bottle does.'—The Doctor, *Too True to be Good*.

'He who has never hoped can never despair.'—Caesar, *Caesar and Cleopatra*.

'And so, to the end of history, murder shall breed murder, always in the name of right and honor and peace, until the gods are tired of blood and create a race that can understand.'—Caesar, *Caesar and Cleopatra*.

'It is not death that matters, but the fear of death.'— Don Juan, *Man and Superman*.

Whoever has intelligently observed the tramp, or visited the ablebodied ward of a workhouse, will admit that our social failures are not all drunkards and weaklings. Some of them are men who do not fit the class they were born into. Precisely the same qualities that make the educated gentleman an artist may make an uneducated manual laborer an ablebodied pauper.—Stage direction in *Man and Superman*.

'When the military man approaches, the world locks up its spoons and packs off its womankind.'—Don Juan, *Man and Superman*.

'There is nothing in Man's industrial machinery but his greed and sloth: his heart is in his weapons . . . Man measures his strength by his destructiveness.'—The Devil, *Man and Superman*.

'Beware the pursuit of the Superman: it leads to an indiscriminate contempt for the Human.'—The Devil, *Man and Superman.*

Joan must be judged a sane woman in spite of her voices because they never gave her any advice that might not have come to her from her mother wit exactly as gravitation came to Newton.—Preface to *Saint Joan.*

Even the selfish pursuit of personal power does not nerve men to the efforts and sacrifices which are eagerly made in pursuit of extensions of our power over nature.—Preface to *Saint Joan.*

The degree of tolerance attainable at any moment depends on the strain under which society is maintaining its cohesion.—Preface to *Saint Joan.*

Mankind, though pugnacious, yet has an instinct which checks it on the brink of selfdestruction.—Preface to *Geneva.*

'It turns out that we do not and cannot love one another—that the problem before us is how to establish peace among people who heartily dislike one another, and have very good reasons for doing so.—Secretary of the League of Nations, *Geneva.*

'Unless the highest court can be set in motion by the humblest individual justice is a mockery.'—The Judge, *Geneva.*

'A man's interest in the world is only the overflow from his interest in himself.'—Captain Shotover, *Heartbreak House.*

'Them she lived with would have killed her for a hat-pin, let alone a hat.'—Eliza, *Pygmalion*.

'I'm one of the undeserving poor: thats what I am.'—Alfred Doolittle, *Pygmalion*.

'The test of a man's or woman's breeding is how they behave in a quarrel. Anybody can behave well when things are going smoothly.'—Craven, *The Philanderer*.

'I'm only a beer teetotaller, not a champagne tee-totaller.'—Prossy, *Candida*.

'You will also learn that when the master has come to do everything through the slave, the slave becomes his master, since he cannot live without him.'—He-Ancient, 'As Far as Thought Can Reach', *Back to Methuselah*.

'. . . it is dangerous to shew too much to people who do not know what they are looking at. I think that a man who is sane as long as he looks at the world through his own eyes is very likely to become a dangerous madman if he takes to looking at the world through telescopes and microscopes.'—Elderly Gentleman, 'Tragedy of an Elderly Gentleman,' *Back to Methuselah*.

'I have the utmost respect, madam, for the magnificent discoveries which we owe to science. But any fool can make a discovery. Every baby has to discover more in the first years of its life than Roger Bacon ever discovered in his laboratory.'—Elderly Gentleman, 'Tragedy of an Elderly Gentleman,' *Back to Methuselah*.

'Flinders Petrie has counted nine attempts at civilisation made by people exactly like us; and every one of them failed just as ours is failing. They failed because the citizens and statesmen died of old age or over-eating before they had grown out of schoolboy games and savage sports and cigars and champagne.'—Conrad Barnabas, 'The Gospel of the Brothers Barnabas,' *Back to Methuselah*.

We must not stay as we are, doing always what was done last time, or we shall stick in the mud. Yet neither must we undertake a world as catastrophic Utopians, and wreck our civilization in our hurry to mend it.—Postscript to *Back to Methuselah*.

'Do not mistake mere idle fancies for the tremendous miracle-working force of Will nerved to creation by a conviction of Necessity. I tell you men capable of such willing, and realizing its necessity, will do it reluctantly, under inner compulsion, as all great efforts are made . . . They will live three hundred years, not because they would like to, but because the soul deep down in them will know that they must, if the world is to be saved.'—Franklyn Barnabas, 'The Gospel of the Brothers Barnabas,' *Back to Methuselah*.

'You cannot have power for good without having power for evil too.'—Cusins, *Major Barbara*.

Optimistic lies have such immense therapeutic value that a doctor who cannot tell them convincingly has mistaken his profession.—Preface to *Misalliance*.

'You can always tell an old soldier by the inside of his holsters and cartridge boxes. The young ones carry pistols and cartridges: the old ones, grub.'—Bluntschli, *Arms and the Man*.

There have been summits of civilisation at which heretics like Socrates, who was killed because he was wiser than his neighbours, have not been tortured, but ordered to kill themselves in the most painless manner known to their judges. But from that summit there was a speedy relapse into our present savagery.—Preface to *On the Rocks*.

In a really civilised state flogging would cease because it would be impossible to induce any decent citizen to flog another.—Preface to *On the Rocks*.

'There are two sorts of people in the world: the people anyone can live with and the people that no one can live with.'—Patricia, *The Millionairess*.

'Oh, the deep end! the deep end! What is life if it is not lived at the deep end?'—Epifania, *The Millionairess*.

'In your time the young were post-Marxists and their fathers pre-Marxists. Today we are all post-Atomists.'—Junius Smith, *Buoyant Billions*.

Prola: 'It is dangerous to educate fools.'
Pra: 'It is still more dangerous to leave them uneducated.'—*The Simpleton of the Unexpected Isles*.

'We shall make wars because only under the strain of war are we capable of changing the world; but the changes our wars will make will never be the changes we intended them to make.'—Prola, *The Simpleton of the Unexpected Isles*.

'What use is bravery now when any coward can launch an atomic bomb? Until men are wise and women civilised they had better not be born. At all events I shall not bring them into this wicked world to kill and be killed.'—Young Woman, *Farfetched Fables* (First Fable).

ON POLITICS AND POLITICIANS

I flatter myself that the unique survival of the Fabian Society among the forgotten wrecks of its rivals, all very contemptuous of it, was due not only to its policy, but in the early days to the one Irish element in its management.— *Sixteen Self-Sketches*.

I had read Karl Marx fourteen years before Lenin did.— Contribution to *Myself and Some Friends*, Lillah McCarthy, 1933.

Mankind, being for the most part incapable of politics, accepts vituperation as an easy and congenial substitute.— Notes to *The Devil's Disciple*.

'Moscow is built on English history, written in London by Karl Marx.'—Boanerges, *The Apple Cart*.

Our dilemma is that men in the lump cannot govern themselves; and yet, as William Morris put it, no man is good enough to be another man's master. We need to be governed, and yet to control our governors.—Preface to *The Apple Cart*.

Democracy, then, cannot be government by the people: it can only be government by consent of the governed.— Preface to *The Apple Cart*.

Neither the rulers nor the ruled understand high politics. They do not even know that there is such a branch of knowledge and political science; but between them they can coerce and enslave with the deadliest efficiency, even to the wiping out of civilisation, because their education as slayers has been honestly and thoroughly carried out.'— Preface to *Back to Methuselah*.

'An election is a moral horror, as bad as a battle except for the blood: a mud bath for every soul concerned in it.'—Franklyn Barnabas, 'The Gospel of the Brothers Barnabas,' *Back to Methuselah*.

'We are not practical politicians. We are out to get something done. Practical politicians are people who have mastered the art of using parliament to prevent anything being done.'—Conrad Barnabas, 'The Gospel of the Brothers Barnabas', *Back to Methuselah*.

A child must begin as a Conservative, and learn later that though it must tolerate change it must do so very critically.—Postscript to *Back to Methuselah*.

'The truth is, these political necessities sometimes turn out to be political mistakes.'—Warwick, *Saint Joan*.

'The only man who had a proper understanding of Parliament was old Guy Fawkes.'—Hipney, *On the Rocks*.

I have seen too many newspapers suppressed and editors swept away, not only in Ireland and India but in London in my time, to be taken in by Tennyson's notion that we live in a land where a man can say the thing he will. There is no such country. But this is no excuse for the extravagances of censorship indulged in by jejune governments of revolutionists, and by Churches who imagine they possess the eternal truth about everything, to say nothing of hereditary autocrats who conceive that they are so by divine right.—Preface to *On the Rocks*.

'I don't know whether what Marx said was right or wrong, because I don't know what he said. But I know that he puts into every man and woman that does read him a conceit that they know all about political economy . . .'—Hipney, *On the Rocks*.

'No country has ever been governed by the consent of the people, because the people object to be governed at all.'—Sir Arthur Chavender, *On the Rocks*.

'Man is a failure as a political animal. The creative forces which produce him must produce something better.' —The Judge, *Geneva*.

'In every nation there must be the makings of a capable council and a capable king three or four times over, if only we knew how to pick them. Nobody has found out how to do it: that is why the world is so vilely governed.'— Charles II, *In Good King Charles's Golden Days*.

I have had occasion often to point out that revolutionary movements attract those who are not good enough for established institutions as well as those who are too good for them.—Postscript to *Androcles and the Lion*.

ON RELIGION, THE CHURCH AND THE SPIRIT

'Anger is a bad counsellor: cast out anger. Pity is sometimes worse: cast out pity. But do not cast out mercy. Remember only that justice comes first.'—Inquisitor, *Saint Joan*.

But that there are forces at work which use individuals for purposes far transcending the purpose of keeping these individuals alive and prosperous and respectable and safe and happy . . . is established by the fact that men will, in the pursuit of knowledge and of social readjustments for which they will not be a penny the better, and are indeed often many pence the worse, face poverty, infamy, exile, imprisonment, dreadful hardship, and death.—Preface to *Saint Joan*.

'What will the world be like when The Church's accumulated wisdom and knowledge and experience . . . are thrust into the kennel by every ignorant laborer or dairymaid whom the devil can puff up with the monstrous self-conceit of being directly inspired from heaven? It will be a world of blood, of fury, of devastation, of each man striving for his own hand . . .'—Inquisitor, *Saint Joan*.

'Must then a Christ perish in torment in every age to save those that have no imagination?'—Bishop of Beauvais, Epilogue to *Saint Joan*

'What is my loneliness, compared with the loneliness of God?'—Joan, *Saint Joan*.

'The Crusader comes back more than half a Saracen.'—Bishop of Beauvais, *Saint Joan*.

Better by far declare the throne of God empty than set a liar and a fool on it.—Preface to *Back to Methuselah*.

'I am not an Agnostic: I am a gentleman.'—The Elderly Gentleman, 'Tragedy of an Elderly Gentleman', *Back to Methuselah*.

'Man need not always live by bread alone. There is something else. We do not yet know what it is; but some day we shall find out; and then we will live on that alone; and there shall be no more digging nor spinning, nor fighting, nor killing.'—Eve, 'In the Beginning,' *Back to Methuselah*.

What happened to Hamlet was what had happened fifteen hundred years before to Jesus. Born into the vindictive morality of Moses he has evolved into the Christian perception of the futility and wickedness of revenge and punishment, founded on the simple fact that two blacks do not make a white. But he is not philosopher enough to comprehend this as well as apprehend it.—Postscript to *Back to Methuselah*.

'Of Life only is there no end; and though of its million starry mansions many are empty and many still unbuilt, and though its vast domain is as yet unbearably desert, my seed shall one day fill it and master its matter to its uttermost confines. And for what may be beyond, the eyesight of Lilith is too short. It is enough that there is a beyond.'— Lilith, *Back to Methuselah*.

'I greatly dislike being contradicted; and the only place where a man is safe from contradiction is the pulpit.'—The Burglar, *Too True to be Good*.

'I've got a soul: dont tell me I havnt. Cut me up and you cant find it. Cut up a steam engine and you cant find the steam. But, by George, it makes the engine go.'—Tarleton, *Misalliance*.

'At every one of those concerts in England you will find rows of weary people who are there, not because they really like classical music, but because they think they ought to like it. Well, there is the same thing in heaven. A number of people sit there in glory, not because they are happy, but because they think they owe it to their position to be in heaven.'—The Statue, *Man and Superman*.

'It is not pleasure that makes life worth living. It is life that makes pleasure worth having. And what pleasure is better than the pleasure of holy living?'—George Fox, *In Good King Charles's Golden Days*.

'To you the universe is nothing but a clock that an almighty clockmaker has wound up and set going for all eternity.'—Kneller, *In Good King Charles's Golden Days*.

'Your Majesty: the world must learn from its artists because God made the world as an artist.'—Kneller, *In Good King Charles's Golden Days*.

'Churches are snares of the divvle.'—George Fox, *In Good King Charles's Golden Days*.

'I hope Mary Magdalen made a good end and was forgiven; though we are nowhere told so. But I should not have asked her into my house.'—Mrs. Basham, *In Good King Charles's Golden Days*.

'. . . but where did the thoughts come from? What puts them into our heads? The preachers say they are whispered by God. Anyhow they are whispered; and I want to know exactly how.'—Maiden 5, *Farfetched Fables* (Sixth and Last Fable).

'The Day of Judgment is not the end of the world, but the end of its childhood and the beginning of its responsible maturity.'—The Angel, *The Simpleton of the Unexpected Isles*.

SHAW ON SHAW

There is a section of one of my prefaces headed with the question 'Better than Shakespear?' But a question is not an affirmation, especially when it is answered as I answered it. —Letter in the *Arts Gazette*, London, and Hearst's Magazine 1920.

I did not at first become a dramatic critic. Your first steps in crime don't go as far as that. I started as a musical critic, or rather as a critic of music, which is not always the same thing.—Speech at London Critics' Circle Annual Luncheon, 1929.

Now I, having this taste for the specific art of acting, regard it as part of my business to provide effective material for it. If you want to flatter me you must not tell me that I have saved your soul by my philosophy. Tell me that, like Shakespear, Molière, Scott, Dumas and Dickens, I have provided a gallery of characters which are realer to you than your own relations and which successive generations of actors and actresses will keep alive for centuries as their *chevaux de bataille.*—*Malvern Festival Book,* 1936.

Instead of planning my plays I let them grow as they came, and hardly ever wrote a page foreknowing what the next page would be.—'My Way with a Play', *The Observer,* 1946.

Now it is quite true that my plays are all talk, just as Raphael's pictures are all paint, Michael Angelo's statues all marble, Beethoven's symphonies all noise . . . The quality of a play is the quality of its ideas.—Letter to the *New Statesman and Nation,* 1950.

I cannot deny that I have got the tragedian and I have got the clown in me; and the clown trips me up in the most dreadful way.—Address to The Royal Academy of Dramatic Art, 1928.

My own aim has been that of the practical dramatist: if anything my eye has been too much on the stage.—Preface to *Plays Unpleasant.*

There are certain questions on which I am, like most Socialists, an extreme Individualist. I believe that any society which desires to found itself on a high standard of integrity of character in its units should organise itself in such a fashion as to make it possible for all men and all women to maintain themselves in reasonable comfort by their industry without selling their affections and their convictions.—Preface to *Plays Unpleasant*.

It was as Punch . . . that I emerged from obscurity.— Preface to *Plays Unpleasant*.

I had not achieved a success; but I had provoked an uproar; and the sensation was so agreeable that I resolved to try again.—Preface to *Plays Unpleasant*.

I declare that the real secret of the cynicism and inhumanity of which shallower critics accuse me is the unexpectedness with which my characters behave like human beings, instead of conforming to the romantic logic of the stage.—Preface to *Mrs. Warren's Profession*.

I have advertised myself so well that I find myself, whilst still in middle life, almost as legendary a person as the Flying Dutchman.—Preface to *Three Plays for Puritans*

When I am writing a play I never invent a plot: I let the play write itself and shape itself, which it always does even when up to the last moment I do not foresee the way out.— Postscript to *Back to Methuselah*.

I never felt inclined to write, any more than to breathe. It never occurred to me that my literary sense was exceptional: I gave everyone credit for it; for there is nothing miraculous in a natural faculty to the man who has it.— *Sixteen Self Sketches*.

Happiness is never my aim. Like Einstein I am not happy and do not want to be happy: I have neither time nor taste for such comas, attainable at the price of a pipeful of opium or a glass of whiskey, though I have experienced a very superior quality of it two or three times in dreams.— *Sixteen Self Sketches*.

'Shaw was full not only of Ibsen, but of Wagner, of Beethoven, of Goethe, and, curiously, of John Bunyan. The English way of being great by flashes: Shakespear's way, Ruskin's way, Chesterton's way, without ever following the inspiration upon which William Morris put his finger when he said that Ruskin could say the most splendid things and forget them five minutes after, could not disguise its incoherence from an Irishman . . . His native pride in being Irish persists in spite of his whole adult career in England and his preference for English and Scottish friends.'—Paragraph in third person suggested by Shaw to Frank Harris for his biography of Shaw. *Sixteen Self Sketches*.

Never had any. Success, in that sense, is a thing that comes to you, and takes your breath away, as it came to Byron and Dickens and Kipling. What came to me was repeated failure. By the time I wore it down I knew too much to care about either failure or success.—Answer to catechism in a journal asking him what was his first real success. *Sixteen Self Sketches*.

Music was so important in my development, that nobody can really understand my art without being soaked in symphonies and operas, in Mozart, Verdi and Meyerbeer, to say nothing of Handel, Beethoven and Wagner, far more completely than in the literary drama and its poets and playwrights.—Letter to St. John Ervine.

She (Ellen Terry) became a legend in her old age; but of that I have nothing to say; for we did not meet, and, except for a few broken letters, did not write; and she never was old to me. Let those who may complain that it was all on paper remember that only on paper has humanity yet achieved glory, beauty, truth, knowledge, virtue, and abiding love.—Preface to the *Ellen Terry–Bernard Shaw Correspondence.*

ON THE ARTS

The material of the dramatist is always some conflict of human feeling with circumstances; so that, since institutions are circumstances, every social question furnishes material for drama. But every drama does not involve a social question, because human feeling may be in conflict with circumstances which are not institutions, which raise no question at all, which are part of human destiny.—*The Humanitarian*, May 1895.

To master Wagner's music dramas is to learn a philosophy.—*The Humanitarian*, 1895 (Shaw on Theatre).

The first natural qualification of an actress who is not a mere puppet, impotent without a producer, is imagination.—Contribution to *Myself and Some Friends*, Lillah McCarthy, 1933.

I had so little taste for the Victorian womanly woman that in my first play I made my heroine throttle the parlour maid. The scandal of that outrage shook the London theatre and its Press to their foundations: an easy feat; for their foundations were only an inch deep and very sandy at that.—Contribution to *Myself and Some Friends*, Lillah McCarthy, 1933.

No plot could restrain Shakespear's dramatic genius any more than the conventions of sonata form could restrain Mozart's; but the resultant incongruities are still there . . . —'My Way with a Play,' *The Observer*, 1946.

An author is an instrument in the grip of Creative Evolution.—Postscript to *Back to Methuselah*, 1934.

'The sculptor must have something of the god in him. From his hand comes a form which reflects a spirit. He does not make it to please you, nor even to please himself, but because he must.'—Arjillax, 'As Far as Thought Can Reach,' *Back to Methuselah*.

'I believe in Michael Angelo, Velasquez and Rembrandt; in the might of design, the mystery of color, the redemption of all things by Beauty everlasting, and the message of Art that has made these hands blessed. Amen. Amen.'— Louis Dubedat, *The Doctor's Dilemma*.

Born actors have a susceptibility to dramatic emotion which enables them to seize the moods of their parts intuitively. But to expect them to be intuitive as to intellectual meaning . . . as well, is to demand powers of divination from them: one might as well expect the Astronomer Royal to tell the time in a catacomb.—Preface to *Plays Unpleasant*.

It is quite possible for a piece to enjoy the most sensational success on the basis of a complete misunderstanding of its philosophy: indeed, it is not too much to say that it is only by a capacity for succeeding in spite of its philosophy that a dramatic work of serious poetic import can become popular.—Preface to *Plays Unpleasant*.

No doubt all plays which deal sincerely with humanity must wound the monstrous conceit which it is the business of romance to flatter.—Preface to *Plays Unpleasant.*

Plot has always been the curse of serious drama, and indeed of serious literature of any kind. It is so out of place there that Shakespear never could invent one.—Foreword to *Cymbeline Refinished.*

'I can paint a woman's beauty; but I cannot measure it in a pint pot. Beauty is immeasurable.'—Kneller, *In Good King Charles's Golden Days.*

'It is a strange fact, your Majesty, that no living man or woman can endure his or her portrait if it tells all the truth about them.'—Kneller, *In Good King Charles's Golden Days.*

'Sir, when a man has the gift of a painter, that qualification is so magical that you cannot think of him as anything else. Who thinks of Leonardo as an engineer? of Michael Angelo as an inventor or a sonneteer?'—Kneller, *In Good King Charles's Golden Days.*

'Man: artists do not prove things. They do not need to. They KNOW them.'—Kneller, *In Good King Charles's Golden Days.*

'Mr. Shakespear would have died of shame to see a woman on the stage. It is unnatural and wrong. Only the most abandoned females would do such a thing.'—Mrs. Basham, *In Good King Charles's Golden Days.*

All my musical self-respect is based on my keen appreciation of Mozart's work. It is still as true as it was before the Eroica symphony existed, that there is nothing better in art than Mozart's best.—*Music in London* (Corno di Bassetto).

There must be a growing number of persons who, like myself, would rather have the Ninth Symphony, even from the purely musical point of view, than all the other eight put together, and to whom, besides, it is religious music, and its performance a celebration rather than an entertainment. I am highly susceptible to the force of all truly religious music, no matter to what Church it belongs; but the music of my own church . . . is to be found in the *Die Zauberflöte* and the Ninth Symphony.—*Music in London* (Corno di Bassetto).

There is no shadow of death anywhere on Mozart's music.—*London Music in 1888–9* (Corno di Bassetto).

The success of Wagner has been so prodigious that to his dazzled disciples it seems that the age of what he called 'absolute' music must be at an end, and the musical future destined to be an exclusively Wagnerian one inaugurated at Bayreuth. All great geniuses produce this illusion. Wagner did not begin a movement: he consummated it. He was the summit of the nineteenth-century school of dramatic music in the same sense as Mozart was the summit (the word is Gounod's) of the eighteenth-century school. And those who attempt to carry on his Bayreuth traditions will assuredly share the fate of the forgotten purveyors of second-hand Mozart a hundred years ago.—*The Perfect Wagnerite* (1898).

The truth is, we are apt to deify men of genius, exactly as we deify the creative force of the universe, by attributing to logical design what is the result of blind instinct. What Wagner meant by 'true Art' is the operation of the artist's instinct, which is just as blind as any other instinct.

Mozart, asked for an explanation of his works, said frankly 'How do I know?' Wagner, being a philosopher and critic as well as a composer, was always looking for moral explanations of what he had created; and he hit on several very striking ones, all different.—*The Perfect Wagnerite* (1898).

To enjoy *Tristan* it is only necessary to have had one serious love affair; and though the number of persons possessing this qualification is popularly exaggerated, yet there are enough to keep the work alive and vigorous.— *The Perfect Wagnerite.*

With the greatest artists, there soon commences an integrating of the points into a continuous whole, at which stage the actress appears to make no points at all, and to proceed in the most unstudied and 'natural' way.—Article on Duse, *Plays and Players: Theatre Essays, June,* 1895.

Don Quixote, Brand, and Peer Gynt are, all three, men of action seeking to realize their ideals in deeds . . . Peer, selfish rascal as he is, is not unlovable. Brand, made terrible by the consequences of his idealism to others, is heroic. Their castles in the air are more beautiful than castles of brick and mortar; but one cannot live in them.— *The Quintessence of Ibsenism,* 1891

Ibsen now lays down the complete task of warning the world against its idols and anti-idols, and passes into the shadow of death, or rather into the splendor of his sunset glory; for his magic is extraordinarily potent in these four plays, and his purpose more powerful. And yet the shadow of death is here; for all four, except *Little Eyolf,* are tragedies of the dead, deserted and mocked by the young who are still full of life.—*The Quintessence of Ibsenism,* 1891.

ON THE SEXES

'I should be a good woman if it wasn't so dull. If you're goodnatured, you get put upon. Who are the good women? Those that enjoy being dull and like being put upon.'—'Sweetie', *Too True to be Good*.

'During the war it was found that sex appeal was as necessary for wounded or shellshocked soldiers as skilled nursing; so pretty girls were allowed to pose as nurses because they could sit about on beds and prevent the men from going mad.'—The Burglar, *Too True to be Good*.

'Well, sir, a man should have one woman to prevent him from thinking too much about women in general.'—The Sergeant, *Too True to be Good*.

'Nowadays men all over the world are as much alike as hotel dinners.'—Lysistrata, *The Apple Cart*.

'Women have to unlearn the false good manners of their slavery before they acquire the genuine good manners of their freedom.'—Mrs. Clandon, *You Never Can Tell*.

'I am a woman; and you are a man, with a slight difference that doesn't matter except on special occasions.' —'A', *Village Wooing*.

'Inexperienced men think there is something wonderful you can get from a woman that you never could get from a man. Hence many unhappy marriages.'—'A', *Village Wooing*.

'. . . what is virtue but the Trade Unionism of the married?'—Don Juan, *Man and Superman*.

'Charles: if I spent one week making money or even thinking about it instead of throwing it away with both hands all my charm would be gone. I should become that dull thing, a plain woman.'—Louise de Kéroualle, *In Good King Charles's Golden Days*.

'The women themselves are worse penances than any priest dare inflict on you. Try Barbara: a week with her is worse than a month in hell.'—Charles II, *In Good King Charles's Golden Days*.

'Advanced views, Julia, involve advanced duties: you cannot be an advanced woman when you want to bring a man to your feet, and a conventional woman when you want to hold him there against his will. Advanced people form charming friendships: conventional people marry.'—Charteris, *The Philanderer*.

'The only way for a woman to provide for herself decently is for her to be good to some man that can afford to be good to her.'—Mrs. Warren, *Mrs. Warren's Profession*.

'You give me a happiness I have never experienced before. But if I marry you all this will cease. If I dont marry you—if you die—if we never meet again, it may last all my life.'—Clementina Buoyant, *Buoyant Billions*.

'Love is like music. Music is very nice: the organist says that when the wickedness of mankind tempts him to despair he comforts himself by remembering that the human race produced Mozart; but the woman who plays the piano all day is a curse. A woman who makes love to you all day is much worse; and yet nothing is lovelier than love up to a point.'—Iddy, *The Simpleton of the Unexpected Isles*.

The sex relation is not a personal relation. It can be irresistibly desired and rapturously consummated between persons who could not endure one another for a day in any other relation.—Letter to Frank Harris.

THE LIFE OF
GEORGE BERNARD SHAW

George Bernard Shaw was born in Synge Street, Dublin, on July 26th, 1856; the only son of as ill-assorted a couple as was ever thrown together in an atmosphere of Irish inconsequence or the pages of Dickens. His mother, Lucinda Elizabeth Gurly, was the daughter of an improvident Irish country gentleman who had married into what Shaw described as 'a genuine county family'. As a result the girl was brought up by her grand aunt with exceptional strictness and with all the ladylike accomplishments, but without fortune to sustain them. At the first opportunity she escaped from her aunt by the only means possible to her, which was marriage.

Her unlikely choice, George Carr Shaw, was a bachelor of forty 'with a squint and a vein of humour which delighted in anti-climax', as his son, fully aware of his humorous inheritance, later put it. His resources proved meagre: part-ownership of a corn mill, far from thriving, and a government pension of £60 a year; and his young wife's tastes and education unfitted her totally for the kind of housekeeping their comparative poverty demanded. The young Shaw, therefore, was brought up in the type of genteel impecuniosity which is galling to ambition and often frustrating to genius. To the end of his life he remembered his beginnings with bitterness, not the less because he had been conscious of richer and more distinguished Shaw relatives (one, Sir Frederick Shaw, was Recorder of Dublin and a member of the Imperial Parliament) in the background. Being a poor relation of the rich, he wrote years later, is 'the very devil'; and 'The adult who has been poor as a child, will never get the chill of poverty out of his bones.'

Yet although his father drank and was despised by his wife, a cold woman even towards her children, the home at No. 1 Hatch Street, to which the Shaws soon moved, had compensations for a developing genius. Shaw's education at local schools was unhelpful. He had all the characteristics of self-educated talent. The home atmosphere of music in particular encouraged this. His mother had a beautiful voice, and her teacher, George Vandaleur Lee, came to share the Shaws' house. There were constant musical gatherings, and by his 'teens Shaw was an enthusiastic reader of operatic scores, with a musical knowledge which was to influence his life and career over a span of some eighty years. At the same time he haunted picture galleries and theatres, and responded to the rational religious discussions in his home, so that his atheism was early ingrained; although a sense of the mystery of life, which he was later to describe in *Man and Superman* as the Life Force, always directed his mind towards a kind of spiritual creativity. It was to inspire perhaps his greatest play, *Saint Joan*, as well as the extraordinarily prophetic theme of creative evolution in *Back to Methuselah*.

'Music was so important in my development,' he wrote to the dramatist and critic St. John Ervine, 'that nobody can really understand my art without being soaked in symphonies and operas, in Mozart, Verdi and Meyerbeer, to say nothing of Handel, Beethoven and Wagner, far more completely than in the literary drama and its poets and playwrights.' His discovery of Wagner, through a youthful reading of the score of *Lohengrin*, was to affect profoundly his outlook as a music critic and even as a dramatist. The influences of both Wagner and Mozart can be traced in the themes and philosophical treatment of a number of his plays.

The other major influence, socialism, sprang also from

these early years. A nurse-maid took him as a child into the heart of the Dublin slums, and the horror of it was never to leave him. His reading, too, helped to shape his politics. 'I am not by nature a good bourgeois any more than Shelley was; and I was a strong Shelleyan long before I ever heard of Ibsen from William Archer,' he wrote. He pointed out too that he had read Karl Marx fourteen years before Lenin did.

The background of his interests was therefore civilised and eclectic, and they widened still further after he left school and entered a Dublin estate office as a junior clerk. Among the friends he then made was Chichester Bell, a relative of Alexander Graham Bell who invented the telephone and of Melville Bell who devised a phonetic script, Visible Speech. Thus was born Shaw's interest in phonetics, to be demonstrated in the character of Professor Higgins in *Pygmalion*.

Shaw's work as a boy clerk began at a salary of eighteen shillings a month. His duties included rent collecting, an experience he was to put to use in his first play, *Widowers' Houses*. But the work hardly stretched his talents and although he remained at it for five years he was chilled by its uncongenial routine. It was with relief that, in 1876, he seized the opportunity to emigrate to England, and for this, as for many of his earlier influences, he was indirectly indebted to Vandaleur Lee. In his childhood, it was Lee who had helped to expand his musical horizons and also, by buying a seaside cottage for the family at Dalkey, first awakened his appreciation of scenic beauty. 'I had only to open my eyes there to see such pictures as no painter could make for me,' he wrote. 'The joy of it has remained with me all my life.' Only in Italy was he to find a pictorial beauty which could similarly 'scorch his veins'. But although his eye was acute it was mental stimulation he most craved, and Lee unwittingly opened the way by writing a book on voice production. Its success so spread

the teacher's fame that he left for London in 1872. As he
had been teaching Shaw's sister Lucy, who had a voice of
great promise, Mrs. Shaw almost immediately followed
him with the girl.

Shaw's father moved with his son into lodgings in Har-
court Street, where they remained until 1876, when Shaw's
other sister, Agnes, died of consumption. He was twenty,
and felt the way was now open to join his mother. He set
sail for London with only the vaguest hopes for the future
or idea of his chosen profession. He would have liked to be
a painter or an opera singer, but although he had published
some letters in the press he had never seriously thought of
writing as a profession. 'I never felt inclined to write, any
more than to breathe . . . for there is nothing miraculous in
a natural faculty to the man who has it.' His own faculty
was so instinctive that it was some time before he realised
it must be his life's work; and even then success came
slowly: 'What came to me was repeated failure. By the
time I wore it down I knew too much to care about either
failure or success.'

It was fortunate that his mother, a tolerant woman, was
at least prepared to give her son a permanent haven, for
Shaw's few early attempts at job-finding flickered out and
he became a largely unpaying guest in the house in Fitzroy
Square. With an integrity not unlike her son's, she had
dropped Lee when she found that in London he was
prostituting his gifts and 'Method' by 'pretending to enable his pupils to sing like Patti in twelve lessons', as Shaw
put it. She became a music instructress at North London
College and a highly successful teacher and singer for
other schools and groups until, in her old age, Shaw was at
last able to provide for her. Lucy, though she never fulfilled her mother's operatic hopes, became a professional
singer with some success in light opera.

In the meantime, Shaw settled down to writing novels
conscientiously and with total lack of success. Between

1880 and 1883 he wrote five: *Immaturity*, *The Irrational Knot*, *An Unsocial Socialist*, *Cashel Byron's Profession* and *Love Among the Artists*, all of which failed to find a publisher, and in the end he abandoned the form for good. They were, nevertheless, full of the sociological and artistic ideas which were later to vivify his plays, for he was already penetrating deep into London political life and also writing a good deal of unpaid, or ill-paid, journalism in connection with it. His first regular music criticism was written as 'ghost' for Lee on *The Hornet*, a journal which soon failed; but his main activities were in political groups, where he early taught himself to become a public speaker with a vein of wit and Irish eloquence which was to last to his ninetieth year.

'I spoke in the streets, in the parks, at demonstrations, anywhere and everywhere possible'; and soon he was becoming prominent as a founder member of the Fabian Society, which was formed in 1884 as a kind of intellectual vanguard of the Labour Party. It was a small, middle-class body with a membership totally out of proportion to its later political influence. From it sprang the English Independent Labour Party, whose first elected Member of Parliament, Keir Hardie, reached the House of Commons eight years later, in 1892. Shaw drafted with Hardie the first Labour Party programme; but long before that he had been the major writing force behind the Fabians, editing the *Fabian News* and writing many of the society's tracts, including the *Labour Manifesto* of 1891. In addition he gave his literary help unstintingly to other members, less facile as writers. His Fabian friends and colleagues included Sidney Webb (later Colonial Secretary in the Labour Government of 1930), his talented wife Beatrice, William Morris, H. G. Wells and Mrs. Annie Besant, the later theosophist.

As he refused all payment for his work for the movement Shaw remained very poor, and he has painted for posterity

an almost Dickensian self-portrait of his scarecrow appearance at the time. Undoubtedly it contributed to the slow
development of his interest in women, although one of
those whom he later captivated and jilted, the artist
Bertha Newcombe, described him as 'a passionless man'.
It was largely true, in the sexual sense; his passion was
mainly for causes, including the wellbeing of people as a
whole, rather than any individual. Yet his compassion (and
later his surreptitious charity) was wide, including not
only human beings of all colours and creeds but animals
who were their major victims. He was a strict vegetarian
as well as a deeply committed anti-vivisectionist for most
of his life. That he was capable of a fairly rare but deeply
conceived sexual passion too was to be shown, much later,
in his fierce and painful emotional entanglement with Mrs.
Patrick Campbell.

Shy, gaunt, though not unsusceptible scarecrow that he
was, he was to evade sexual relationships until 1885,
when at the age of twenty-nine he responded to the advances of a young widow, Mrs. Jennie Patterson. Undoubtedly she gave him confidence, and the new Shaw
of the sparkling Irish personality and deliberately Mephistophelean charm was born. Thereafter there were a number of philandering adventures, including a brief comedy
with William Morris's lovely daughter May, who con-
founded Shaw by marrying someone else while he was
still indulging in uncharacteristic romantic dreams about
a mystic, unspoken engagement between them. But by
the time his attraction for women reached an active stage,
success was at last beginning to beckon; rather feebly, for
some years, on the financial side, but enough for notoriety
as critic and socialist propagandist to have stamped the
Shaw image, flame-haired and garrulous, on the public
mind.

It was an entirely conscious image, carefully built up by
Shaw's natural talent for publicity. He had grown tired

of poverty, and with reason, for in 1885, at the age of twenty-nine, he claimed his earnings had still only reached the sum of £117 0s. 3d. that year. Yet the year was a turning point in his career.

William Archer, translator of Ibsen and a well-known dramatic critic, first encountered Shaw in the British Museum Reading Room, Shaw's daily haunt, poring over a French translation of Karl Marx's *Capital* with the score of Wagner's *Tristan and Isolde* open on the table beside it. Perhaps this very incongruity of study attracted the dour but not totally humourless Scot. He took the impecunious young man in hand and soon arranged for him to succeed him as art critic on the *World*. The life-long friendship was later to prove fecund in a more important way, for it was Archer who first suggested to Shaw that he should write plays and introduced him to those of Ibsen, which were to be a main inspiration of Shaw's talent. When the *World* was taken over by a woman, who began revising and rewriting his articles in order to praise the paintings of her friends, Shaw promptly resigned, even though the £2 a week the position provided was his only regular source of income. A period as book reviewer on the *Pall Mall Gazette* was also brief, though years later he was to write much for that journal. But on January 17th, 1888, with T. P. O'Connor as editor, there appeared on the London scene a new evening newspaper, the *Star*, and the following day Shaw was engaged as a leader-writer. He had been suggested to O'Connor by his chief assistant, H. W. Massingham, later first editor of the *New Statesman and Nation*. The liberal O'Connor, however, had not bargained for the red-hot socialism which poured from his new leader-writer's pen, and Shaw was quickly relegated to the columns devoted to music, where it was innocently assumed his ideas could do no harm. It was under the pseudonym he then took, Corno di Bassetto (the Italian name for a defunct musical instrument, the basset horn), that

Shaw made his first serious impact on critical journalism; and basically serious his music articles were, in spite of the wit and sparkle with which he deliberately invested them. Shaw set out to achieve reforms in almost every branch of opera, not only of the general level of singing (and his life with Lee had made him, with his natural musical 'ear', an acute judge of vocal technicalities) but in standards of staging, rehearsal, orchestral playing and acting. Following Wagner, he was interested in opera as a dramatic form which could be judged by the highest standards of the theatre; and it was an essential part of his crusading and forward-looking spirit that the hackneyed operatic repertoire of the time should be attacked so that Wagner's works, still practically ignored at Covent Garden, should be staged as works leading to a new, more robust and intelligent musical future.

Shaw's other great musical passion, Mozart, was in the 1880s and 90s almost as much in need of critical support as Wagner, and in championing the cause his taste was ahead of his time. Music as a whole, not only opera, was fluently covered by Shaw's enthusiastic or vitriolic pen. The bad artist and the bad composer were ever his target, and his judgment on the whole has proved sound by modern standards. In the same way that his playwriting, with its lucid character-descriptions and stage directions, was to revolutionise the publication of plays so that they could be read almost like novels, his music criticism, free from technical jargon, set new standards of readability. Informed without being dull, often riotously funny, it fills four published volumes and enjoys an immortality that is rarely the lot of journalism.

After two years Shaw left the *Star* to take the more lucrative post of music critic on the *World*, now under a new editor. For this he received the good salary, for those days, of five guineas a week, and he only gave up the post in 1894 when offered six guineas by Frank Harris to switch to dramatic criticism on the *Saturday Review*. Although the overlapping of musical and dramatic events in London made it impossible for him to return to music reviewing, Shaw contributed freelance music articles to various papers later and never lost touch or interest. *The Perfect Wagnerite*, published in 1898, the year of publication of his *Plays, Pleasant and Unpleasant*, remains one of the finest studies of Wagner's *Ring* cycle, a classic of its kind.

As a music critic Shaw was enough of a noted figure to attract the attention of Ellen Terry, who first wrote to him on behalf of a young musical protégé whose work she wanted him to see and review. From this sprang the 'paper friendship' with the actress that has been preserved in a famous volume of letters, *Ellen Terry and Bernard Shaw: A Correspondence* (1931). Shaw's new position as dramatic critic considerably enhanced his reputation. 'The drama being a much less segregated cult than music, my fame at once increased with a rush', he wrote in *Sixteen Self Sketches*; and as he was a born crusader his pen turned from championship of Wagner to the equally underrated and derided Ibsen.

In a sense, Shaw's outlook on drama could be neither as catholic nor as objective as on music. He was already, in 1894, a playwright himself following in Ibsen's footsteps, and to get a hearing either for himself or his idol it was necessary to wrench playgoers away not only from the popular and worthless theatre fare of the day but also from Shakespeare at the Lyceum Theatre. Shaw's attacks on Shakespeare have been exaggerated and misunderstood. He rejected him as a political or social thinker, because it was necessary to establish these new dramatic ideas. But he was also perceptive enough to attack the mutilations of the plays in Sir Henry Irving's productions, and this made him a champion of the production reforms of William Poel, which gave the plays nearly in full, with the Elizabethan fluency of action. He was insistent on the need to bring out the natural music and imagery of the verse, and he was a superb and imaginative judge of acting, his study of Forbes-Robertson's Hamlet remaining memorable. Although he preferred Forbes-Robertson and was harsh about some of Irving's 'personality' interpretations, thinking them untrue to Shakespeare, he was also fully aware of his talents and 'distinction'. Shaw's perception was to be proved later in the production of his own plays, where he won the admiration of the distinguished players he handled at rehearsal, from Granville Barker to Sybil Thorndike. He was, according to many of them, 'a born actor'.

His main critical interest, however, centred on the 'iron-mouthed Ibsen', for here lay the roots of his own genius. As a dramatist of ideas Shaw could not match Ibsen's psychological subleties and depth, but with greater wit he was to carry his social analyses into wider ranges of human thought and society. His debt is crystallised in *The Quintessence of Ibsenism*, first published in 1891 and revised in 1913 to cover the last four plays.

1913 was the year of Shaw's own *Pygmalion*. He had become, since *The Quintessence of Ibsenism* was first published, a fully established and world-famous dramatist. He had begun, abortively, writing plays in 1885, when he collaborated (or, rather, failed to collaborate) with William Archer on a play in which Archer was supposed to supply the dramatic construction and Shaw the dialogue. The project was abandoned when it became obvious that Archer (later the author of a popular melodrama, *The Green Goddess*) was a romantic who could not survive in Shaw's world of astringent social irony. But in 1891 J. T. Grein founded the new Independent Theatre as a channel for the plays of Ibsen, and during a long walk, which began in the Hammersmith Road at midnight and ended many hours later, Shaw pointed out to Grein that if his organisation was to have any lasting influence it must find new plays by new British dramatists. He proposed himself to fill the gap, and for the purpose completed *Widowers' Houses*, the play he had begun with Archer seven years before. Presented by the Independent Theatre Society at the Royalty for a single performance on December 9th, 1892, and repeated on December 13th, it was his first play to reach the stage, and his whole subsequent career grew out of it. This was two years before he became a dramatic critic, and as Shaw subsequently wrote, 'I had not achieved a success; but I had provoked an uproar; and the sensation was so agreeable that I resolved to try again.'

The result was *The Philanderer*, a comedy based partly on himself in that rôle and including character sketches of two of his mistresses, Jennie Patterson and Florence Farr, the actress. The comedy's emphasis on sexual freedom makes it read and act with surprising vitality today; but at the time it proved unstageable and did not achieve a public run until 1907 at the Royal Court Theatre. *Mrs. Warren's Profession*, written in 1893 and 1894, also had very delayed production, as it dealt with the social factors behind prostitution. But in 1898 Shaw published the trilogy as the 'unpleasant' section of *Plays, Pleasant and Unpleasant*, the 'pleasant' being represented by *Arms and the Man*, *Candida*, *The Man of Destiny* and *You Never Can Tell*.

Arms and the Man had been first presented by Florence Farr for a brief, unsuccessful London run in 1894, but like *Candida* has had prolonged success in the theatre to the present day. Shaw's first financial success was *The Devil's Disciple*, a comedy melodrama which happened to suit the talents of a popular American actor, Richard Mansfield, who staged it in New York in 1897. It was still running in May, 1898, when he gave up his post as dramatic critic and allowed himself, the following month, to marry a wealthy Irish heiress, Charlotte Payne-Townshend. 'Not until I was past forty', he wrote to Frank Harris, 'did I earn enough to marry without seeming to marry for money.'

Shaw had first met Charlotte in 1896, at one of Beatrice Webb's country house weekends. Although the friendship had ripened, Shaw, who was happy in his bachelorhood, resisted marriage because of this sensitivity about seeming to marry for money. He was, however, attracted and tended to dance like a moth around the flame. Charlotte, green-eyed and rather piquant, was also almost forty. She had had an abortive attachment to the writer Alex Munthe, but the Fabians, who, as policy, liked their supporters to marry money, had not been able to match her to any of the members they threw in her way. Her parents' home life had been unhappy, and, as subsequently appeared, she had an inhibition about bearing children. Her use to the Fabians had already been considerable. She had donated £1,000 to the Library of the London School of Economics and founded a woman's scholarship. Her flat at 10, Adelphi Terrace, was over the School. She was attracted to Shaw, and an accident opened the way to her marrying him. Shaw had suffered a slight foot injury which in 1898 developed into a painful disability, making his visits to the theatre a burden. Charlotte was in Rome at the time, but his letters about his injury alarmed her sufficiently to make her rush back to London. Appalled by the conditions she found in his study (Shaw refused to allow servants to dust the room or disturb his papers), she insisted that he join her in the country air near Haslemere; and to Shaw, in the circumstances, marriage was the only answer.

They were married on June 1st, 1898, with the bridegroom on crutches. He was almost forty-two years old. Although after his wife's death he confessed he was the type of person, totally absorbed in his work, who should never have married, the long years they spent together were by no means unpleasant. It was a strange and entirely celibate union, Shaw later admitted to St. John Ervine. This was at Charlotte's own insistence; but her possessive jealousy was strong and of considerable concern to Shaw in his later infatuation with Mrs. Pat Campbell. Charlotte helped him in many ways, and has earned her place in literary history by first interesting Shaw in the trial of Joan of Arc.

Shaw's political activities never totally ceased. By the time of his marriage he was serving on St. Pancras Borough Council, then known as St. Pancras Vestry. In 1904 he stood unsuccessfully as Labour candidate for the London County Council, and as a Borough Councillor he wrote *The Commonsense of Municipal Trading*, which was highly regarded. In the fields of education and public health, in particular, his influence was forward-looking and lasting.

Total acceptance as a dramatist in England did not come until 1905, when *Man and Superman* was produced at the Royal Court Theatre, achieving a run of 176 performances and giving the English language a new and recognisable phrase. The Royal Court Theatre was, in fact, to be the pivot of Shaw's career. The management had been formed by a good businessman, J. E. Vedrenne, in association with the actor-producer Granville Barker as artistic director, and it was to last for four years. Barker had acted in Shaw's plays, and although young enough to be Shaw's son had developed a strong affinity with him. He and the Court provided the Shaw plays with opportunities for public performance hitherto largely denied them, and this certainty of production stimulated Shaw himself into a period of high creativity.

The Court staged the shortened version of *Man and Superman*, with Barker as John Tanner and his then wife, Lillah McCarthy, as Ann Whitefield. In 1907 the omitted Act III was performed under the title of *Don Juan in Hell* for a series of eight matinées. *John Bull's Other Island*, *Major Barbara* and *You Never Can Tell* also achieved popularity at the Court. The last of the major plays written for the theatre and produced there was *The Doctor's*

Dilemma. In April, 1907, Shaw wrote a letter to Barker pointing out that the venture had run its full course and advising him to take over the management of the Savoy Theatre, where Barker proceeded to build up a reputation as a Shakespearean producer. The breaking-up of his marriage to Lillah McCarthy finally severed his relationship with Shaw. His new American wife disliked Shaw and influenced Barker to leave the theatre and devote himself to writing. To Shaw this was a personal blow of which only his closest friends were fully aware, for the attractive and talented young actor had begun to take the place of a son. When, as an old man in 1946, he heard on the wireless the news of Barker's death in Paris, it was still capable of giving him a pang.

Three years before he had written to Barker the news of Charlotte's death. 'She had not forgotten you. It was a blessedly happy ending, but you could not have believed I should be as deeply moved. You will not, I know, mind my writing this to you. She was 86. I am 87. GBS.' It was a feeler into the affectionate past, written in loneliness; but there is no indication that Barker responded. At his death he was sixty-eight years old, and forty years had passed since the golden days of achievement at the Royal Court.

In 1913 a business correspondence with Mrs. Pat Campbell about *Pygmalion*, in which Shaw wanted her to play Eliza, suddenly flared into an infatuation which was the first and last of its kind in his life. He admired her as an actress, and some years before had written *Caesar and Cleopatra* for her and Forbes-Robertson. It is perhaps significant that Shaw could think of her as Eliza, although she was forty-nine, and it is certainly a tribute to her personal magic that she played the part with effect; but in the meantime Shaw's letters suddenly burst into Irish hyperbole, only half in fun now and shot with Celtic anguish. His concern for Charlotte's own anguish remained, and how far the affair actually went can still only be conjecture. He certainly photographed his enchantress in bed, quite naturally provoking speculation as to what he was doing in the bedroom. The crisis, however, was reached when he followed her to Sandwich and, leaving a note full of alarm, she ran away before he arrived. There is no doubt that he suffered, and not only in pride. But he was fifty-six; old enough to recover and put business concerns before emotional ones. Right at the end of rehearsals the first Eliza created chaos in the theatre by taking leave of absence without warning to marry George Cornwallis-West and go on honeymoon with him; but everything, in true theatre tradition, was 'all right on the night', and *Pygmalion*, with Sir Herbert Beerbohm Tree as Higgins, was launched on its long career of success. To the end, Mrs. Pat was to be a rose with a thorn to Shaw. Her total irresponsibility and the loss of her Italianate beauty finally wrecked her career, and she intensified her appeals to be permitted to publish Shaw's letters (America had offered her a large sum for them). He would never allow it in Charlotte's lifetime, and Charlotte outlived her rival. In the end they were published only to further the education of Mrs. Pat's grandchildren. But in her last year in France, shortly before her death, he sent her a cheque for £4,000. No one knew of it until some years after his death. Shaw's other generosities, which included help to young actors and writers and the private subsidising of Arnold Dolmetsch's festivals with his early musical instruments at Haslemere were equally secret and unobtrusive. He had the very rare gift, St. John Ervine has said, of giving without being asked.

The first world war saw Shaw active as a writer against its imbecilities and loss of life, but creatively he did not revive until *Heartbreak House*, begun in 1913 but completed only after the war. This Chekhovian tragi-comedy of a society disintegrating still carries its message in every world crisis. It is a vehicle for atmosphere and fine acting,

Captain Shotover being one of Shaw's greatest creations. He thought it his best play. *Saint Joan*, in 1924, was written after he discovered the ideal actress in Sybil Thorndike. Closely based on historical records, it was the first and finest of the modern theatre translations of history and the forces behind it into contemporary terms. In the meantime there had been the astonishing five-play cycle of *Back to Methuselah*, a panorama of human society beginning in the Garden of Eden and ending far into the future. First staged by Barry Jackson at Birmingham Repertory Theatre, with a cast including Edith Evans and Cedric Hardwicke, it only fully established its stage viability in 1969 when a production at the National Theatre, influenced by the space age, accentuated its timeless topicality.

In 1929 a comedy of kingship, *The Apple Cart*, again with Cedric Hardwicke and Edith Evans, had a long West End run and helped to establish Jackson's Malvern Festival, devoted mainly to Shaw, as a regular feature of the summers of the 1930s. The Edith Evans part, Orinthia, was based on Mrs. Pat, who heard of the project and revived the Shaw correspondence with wails of unsuccessful protest. The Festivals and Shaw's best creativity ended in 1939 at the outbreak of war, when his new historical play, *In Good King Charles's Golden Days*, showed that the octogenarian could still command dialogue and character which could hold the stage without incident yet with a fluent grasp of eloquence and ideas. In this surprising play, King Charles II, his Court ladies, Sir Isaac Newton and George Fox, the Quaker, are thrown together in a cauldron of thought which coalesces both their creative ideas and the fallibilities of their arguments in the light of modern scientific knowledge.

One ill-regarded play of the early 'thirties, *Too True to Be Good*, has proved in recent revival, both in New York and London, to have had a remarkably prophetic insight into less realistic stage techniques and apocalyptic war. Its ideas, including the generation gap and rejection of family relationships, are far closer to social truths of our own time than when it was written. The play was split down the middle, as were so many, by Shaw's inability not to play the fool. 'I cannot deny that I have got the tragedian and I have got the clown in me; and the clown trips me up in the most dreadful way', as he once confessed. It was the quality of sheer fun which caused Mrs. Pat to address him as 'Joey'. A character, Private Meek, based on the Shaws' close friend, Lawrence of Arabia, is the best feature of the comedy in the play.

Shaw never stopped writing: he was, as he said, 'a writing machine'. Two short books of his prime were *The Intelligent Woman's Guide to Socialism and Capitalism* (1928), a potent encouragement of women in political thinking, and the 'fable' *The Adventures of the Black Girl in Her Search for God* (1932), an attempt to clarify religious thinking which provoked an uproar in the critical press but sold over 200,000 copies within a year. One of the last of his fifty-one plays, *Buoyant Billions*, was written in 1946 and 1948, when he was over ninety, and produced in London in 1949. It is a minor but not totally negligible work, a repeat of earlier ideas on Life Force and marriage but with a potent opening discussion of the new world created by the atom bomb. This line of thought he continued in *Farfetched Fables*, a futuristic study like *Back to Methuselah* and in some ways a remarkable vision for a ninety-two-year-old. To the end, in the columns of newspapers and journals he continued to write sense, with undiminished wit.

He had studies both in the house and garden of his home in Ayot St. Lawrence, Hertfordshire, and here his last years were mainly spent. It was peace for him after the activities of the 'thirties, when Charlotte, who loved travel, dragged him about the world against his inclination, and when the ferment of politics still drew him into controversies. His play *Geneva*, guying the dictators Hitler (Battler) and Mussolini (Bombardone) was a great success in 1938 but he grew to hate it. The view that he supported these dictators, in particular Mussolini, is a curious twisting of fact, but it gained some credence owing to his visit with Lady Astor and others to Soviet Russia and from some remarks about the fallacies of democratic rule, in which as he pointed out the people as a whole do not take part and rarely actively influence events: there must always be those to govern, with specific safeguards. In this view he was honest, somewhat shrewd, but often misinterpreted; but Shaw's human compassion and hatred of cruelty in all forms made it impossible for him to vindicate the savageries dictatorship threw up, or its dreams of national military glory, as his writings show. In politics he was a socialist to the end, in the wider Marxian meaning of the word. Outside the theatre he was always vivaciously aware of new inventions and media, and he became an expert broadcaster as well as being, for a time, an ex-officio member of the B.B.C's General Advisory Council.

In the 'twenties and 'thirties he developed a lasting friendship, little known until long after his death, with a young American actress, Molly Tompkins, who engaged his susceptible imagination to the age of ninety without the intrusive emotions of earlier entanglements. It was a light flirtation, no more, in which he was charitable and helpful, and it left behind, like the stormier Mrs. Pat affair and the warmly distant Ellen Terry one, a correspondence that reads engagingly. It was the last dying ember of The Philanderer, whose conquests had nearly always been, like the Ellen Terry one, 'on paper'. 'Let those who may complain that it was all on paper remember that only on paper has humanity yet achieved glory, beauty, truth, knowledge, virtue, and abiding love,' he wrote after Ellen Terry's death.

At the age of ninety-four he fell in the garden at Ayot St. Lawrence in attempting to prune a tree, breaking a thigh bone. After a spell in Luton Hospital, he insisted on being brought back to his home, where he died on November 2nd, 1950. Theatres on Broadway extinguished their lights. He had refused all honours, except the Nobel Prize for Literature in 1925, because of his democratic principles, and he was not, as some hoped he would be, buried in Westminster Abbey. Instead, his ashes were scattered with Charlotte's in his own garden.